Hearts Set on the Pilgrimage

1680 373RD AVE NE
STANCHFIELD, MN 55080

ALSO BY JOAN PULS, O.S.F.

Every Bush Is Burning
A Spirituality for Our Times

A Spirituality of Compassion

JOAN PULS

HEARTS SET ON THE PILGRIMAGE

The Challenge of Discipleship in a World Church

XXIII
TWENTY-THIRD PUBLICATIONS
Mystic, Connecticut

Twenty-Third Publications
185 Willow Street
P.O. Box 180
Mystic, CT 06355
(203) 536-2611

ISBN 0-89622-403-1
Library of Congress Catalog Card Number 89-51385

DEDICATION

To the Community of St. Ben's

Contents

Introduction

Flight 297 left Heathrow Airport at 2:15 P.M. headed for Chicago. Above the clouds in clear sunlight I gazed out at the vast expanse of surrounding sky. My thoughts drifted to fragments of Psalm 19: "The heavens declare the glory of God....Through all the earth their voice resounds, and to the ends of the world, their message." The skies have become our highways, linking peoples and worlds and experiences. I had just finished another phase of my ecumenical journey, a six-month sojourn in Britain, in a small ecumenical community in a little village in Norfolk. From there I had visited communities in the Lake District, in London, in Birmingham, in York, in Sussex, and in Wales, where I had tasted church life and engaged with other searching Christians. My preoccupation during these recent months had been the slow emergence of an ecumenical spirituality that will, I hope, serve the purposes of God in our contemporary world.

Renewal is an uneven process, I have found in these past five years of global ecumenical activities. Karl Rahner described our present situation as "one of transition from a church sustained by a homogeneously Christian society and almost identical with it, to a church made up of those who have struggled against their environment in order to reach a personally clear and explicitly responsible decision of faith." "This," he says, "will be the church of the future, or there will be no church at all."[1] What if, I have asked myself, the best dreams of Vatican II, of numerous recent ecumenical conferences, of brave new ecumenical projects, of religious orders in their serious renewal efforts, were to converge? What is the message of today's Pentecost? What is being asked of Christian communities, of each of us as disciples, as the twentieth century becomes the twenty-first?

In the following chapters, I attempt to describe an ecumenical spirituality that might hasten and nurture this emerging church. My reflections have grown out of experiences with the world church, in places as varied as Yugoslavia, Canada, India, the USA, and western Europe. My own bias as a Westerner is obvious, though I have benefitted greatly from contacts with a global church and especially with personal friends from a wide variety of traditions and backgrounds. I am deeply indebted to the World Council of Churches for some of my more comprehensive education and to many individuals and communities in England who have most recently shared this exploration of an ecumenical spirituality. My deepest thanks go to my religious community which has endorsed and enabled my continued journey, and to Gwen Cashmore, my ecumenical partner in searching and living this vision.

Throughout the following pages, I echo a call to faithfulness, to the gospels, to the best of our Christian history and tradition, to those moments of Pentecost we have all experienced. I affirm that the church belongs to the people of God, to the laity as well as clergy, to women as well as men, to all who sincerely seek truth and life. This is a time for reassessing our Christian vocation as ordained ministers, as persons with authority, as adult Christians. Therefore, I offer this book especially to those who believe that small ecumenical communities are the hope of a renewed Christian presence in our world today.

One longs to see the church becoming in modest, minor, broken ways something of a paradigm, a model . . . of what grace can bring about—a fellowship of the "unlike" able to speak to the world of the possibility of genuine reconciliation and justice because its members have begun to realize in their own life together the radical implications of God's reconciliation.[2]

The themes and images I have chosen describe, I believe, that kind of fellowship, that kind of reconciling community. It will be a pilgrim church, a servant church, marked by its hospitality. It will be a reconciling and a prophetic church, open to inevitable suffering. It will herald good news, as it remembers, celebrates, and gives thanks. I am aware that these themes have been treated more fully elsewhere, and I claim as my inspiration numerous church visionaries: Leonardo Boff, Walter Brueggeman, Rosemary Haughton, Kosuke Koyama, Lesslie Newbigin, Philip Potter, Dorothee Sölle, John V. Taylor. . . .

If my reflections challenge other small communities to raise questions of their own renewal, and if they encourage groups of Christians to persevere in their search for an ecumenical spirituality that will sustain and nourish them, their mission will be accomplished. It is through the witness of each of us that the priestly prayer of Jesus will be made incarnate, "To them I have revealed your name, and I will continue to reveal it, so that your love for me may live in them, and I may live in them" (John 17:26).

Hearts Set on the Pilgrimage

It was the end of a four-day ecumenical retreat. We were gathered in the dining room, well into our closing service. Earlier, in the garden, we had heard Abraham's summons (and ours): "Go forth to a land that I will show you" (Genesis 12:1). Now Rosemary held up the golden-brown loaf she had baked that morning. Two others helped her break and distribute it. "Pilgrim bread for pilgrim people" reverberated around the room as we shared bread and peace, thanksgiving for the journey begun and blessings for the journey to be resumed.

Later that day three of us traveled south to Birmingham. The weather had thickened into rain and fog. Friday evening traffic was heavy and impatient. We exited at Bromsgrove junction and headed into the countryside. We turned onto a narrower road. Suddenly lights ahead beckoned to us and guided us up a hill onto a spacious driveway. We had arrived, weary and relieved, at the Community of Reconciliation. Moments later we were sitting around the table with other travelers and with the resident community, breaking bread together and giving thanks for safe journeys and for refuge. Pilgrim bread for pilgrim people!

Is this not what the Eucharist is meant to be? I asked myself that night. Is this not the meaning of Jesus' admonition: Do this in memory of me? Is this not the basis of our experience each time we approach the table? A meal for pilgrims, who are bound together by common yearnings, en route to a community, a church, that stretches into God's reign itself?

Vatican II gave Roman Catholics like myself a fresh image for the church of Jesus Christ:

> However until there be realized new heavens and a new earth in which justice dwells, the pilgrim church, in its sacraments and institutions, which belong to this present age, carries the mark of this world which will pass, and she herself takes her place among the creatures which groan and travail yet and await the revelation of the sons [children] of God.[1]

Out of the ecclesiastical rhetoric, there shines a description of church as pilgrim. In contrast to the centuries of triumphalism. In harmony with the frailty and muddled search of wayfarers. For that is what we are, pilgrims, wending our way, awaiting, even as we seek and discover, our real identity as children of God, members of one body.

"The pilgrim church...carries the mark of this world which will pass...." As Christians we reflect regularly on the journey our ancestors made. Salvation history is the unfolding of a pilgrim march out of Haran, into Egypt, into the desert, down through centuries of enslavement and exploitation, of purging and testing, of repeated infidelities and repeated renewals of the covenant. The symbol of that journey, interrupted and resumed, was the daytime cloud and the nighttime pillar of fire.

The ancient prayers of God's people reflected their pilgrim status. Moses sang: "In your mercy you led the people you redeemed. In your strength you guided them to your holy dwelling" (Exodus 15:13). In her canticle of joy, Hannah prayed: "The Lord will guard the footsteps of the faithful ones" (1 Samuel 2:9). And the Psalmist echoed: "Happy those whose strength you are! Their hearts are set upon the pilgrimage" (Psalm 84:6). "My journeys and my rest you scrutinize....where can I go from your spirit? . . . see if my way is crooked and lead me in the way of old" (Psalm 139: 3, 7, 24).

Isaiah announced God's reign in pilgrim terms: "A highway will be there called the holy way....it is for those with a journey to make, and on it the redeemed will walk" (Isaiah 35:8-9). Hosea spoke of God's maternal love: "It was I who taught Ephraim to walk" (Hosea 11:3). John the Baptist joined the stream of prophets and preachers: "Prepare the way of the Lord. Make straight his paths" (Matthew 3:3). And the first words Jesus' disciples heard addressed to them were a call to be pilgrims: "Come, follow me" (John 1:39). They were commissioned as such: "He instructed them to take nothing on their journey" (Mark 6:8). Jesus often used the traveling image in his parables: the prodigal son, the good Samaritan, the head of the house setting out on a journey.

The gospels read as a travel narrative, from village to village, to the mountain top, to the desert, across the lake, into foreign territories, on the road to Jerusalem. Jesus' final injunction before he handed himself over was, "Come, then! Let us be on our way" (John 14:31). Jesus required that his followers be pilgrims, leaving their nets and the dead to be buried, trusting in God's providence, availing themselves to strangers, foregoing permanent resting places and the stability and status of position and salary. Jesus was the way. His disciples were sent on that way, to bear fruit. All his resurrection messages include the message: Go...to my brothers (and sisters); go...tend my sheep; go...into Galilee; go...and make disciples; go...into the whole world.

What happens when we affirm the notion of the church as a pilgrim church? We re-invoke an incarnational principle, the Word become flesh, and we relive that pilgrimage of divestment and identification. God is Emmanuel, companion with us on the way. The world becomes the arena for God's action and God's grace. Human history and human existence become the locus for our discovery of our relationship to one another and to the God of us all. "In every place where you find the imprint of human feet, there am I."[2] The pilgrim nature of the church enables us and entitles us to integrate our earthly and heavenly journeys into an interconnected, entwined, single journey. We are a people called to live here and now the life that God intends for us, even while we seek the fullness of its gifts and its glory.

But what does it mean, in our world today, to be a pilgrim church that groans and travails, as we move toward a new heaven and a new earth? It means, first of all, the freedom within and without, to journey. Both are important. The unknown is threatening to most of us. We experience it every time we set ourselves to learn a new skill, a new language, to embark on a new job, a new chapter of our lives. I recently learned how to drive with a stick shift. For years automatic driving has been natural to me and enjoyable. I hardly think twice about effort or risk. I am free to come and go, in all weathers and climes. When I was confronted with this new challenge, I was unfree and unwilling. It was a journey I wanted to refuse. It meant diminishment and beginner status, taxed concentration, and possible failure. Only when I achieved a degree of inner freedom was there any possibility of my becoming adept with gears and clutch.

As a people, living our faith as mature and dynamic Christians can be very threatening. We know what we've been taught. We are comfortable in our prosaic practices and familiar rituals. So much easier not to critically reflect, not to question authority, not to take our own discoveries too seriously. We are shocked when a fresh interpretation breaks through our rigid categories, when persons we are getting to know, or whom we respect, act and think unexpectedly, when we find ourselves in a foreign setting forced to respond creatively and spontaneously. That is when we know how free we are within, to journey onward. So much awaits exploration, so much can be learned and mutually exchanged. There are virtually no limits to a faith released into the freedom of God's own Spirit.

I knew Michael Cullen in 1969 when he was released from jail. He had served a nine months sentence for breaking a law, entering a Selective Service office and burning draft files. He had not always been a war resister. He was a seminarian from Ireland who found his way out of clergy-training into providing shelter for the homeless. On the streets he quickly saw the incongruence between the plight of the poor and national defense policies. Michael's pilgrimage led to prison and then to deportation. Fifteen years later, he and his wife Nettie, with their twelve children, are converting an old monastic foundation near Dublin into a retreat center and a camp for teenagers. It began, Michael says, when they made a decision to give up two years of their life to serve the cause of the poor. But the two years became a pilgrimage. Michael and Nettie's story is key to our own. Faith was concretized. Faith enough to make a concrete decision. Faith enough to follow where led.

We travel as a people, as a church. Therefore we need to free one another for the journey. The helping hand of freedom from without comes in a variety of guises. As family and friends, we support each other on our individual and common journeys. We help clear the way for one another. We become co-discerners of that way. As communities, we hope to challenge and inspire each other to probe, to wrestle with, and to embody our professions of faith. As persons with authority—especially authority understood as the ability to encourage and enable others—we bless one another's pilgrimage, we create as much space as possible for the Spirit to work. And we refrain from defining the route too explicitly or determining the validity of one another's revelations.

A pilgrim church assists its youth in their groping and their experiments with truth and freedom. It remains fluid and flexible enough for them to exercise their creative imaginations and test their ideas within its compassionate and trusting embrace. A pilgrim church opens itself to the correction and the insights of others, dialogues rather than competes, finds avenues for joint witness rather than glories in its own accomplishments. A pilgrim church journeys together in human patterns of participation and exchange rather than in hierarchical or top-heavy structures. It is the Taizé community, in France, with its open fields and tents, its youth-directed counseling, its all-night prayer vigils. It is Cardinal Arns and Bishop Lorscheider walking with Leonardo Boff to a Roman inquiry. It is South African clergy sharing their people's struggles, risking their own lives, and redeeming the days of ecclesiastical neutrality. It is Roman Catholic sisters imprisoned with other peacemakers, and lay men and women leading others in the spiritual life. It is your pilgrim friends and mine who show us the meaning of hospitality, detachment, and risk.

Pilgrims forego the security of roots and the status of established residents. They live in the insecurity of faith and the uncertainty of an indefinite destination. They obey the promptings and urgings of the Spirit. They are part of that "cloud of witnesses" who keep their eyes fixed on Jesus and the new community he proclaimed. They have a conviction and a confidence about things unseen and about things made known to them along the way.

Being a pilgrim church also means the willingness to travel light, carrying only essentials, living off the land, accepting the hospitality of others. It means sharing what is available with companions and strangers. Often during recent years I find myself packing a suitcase. I have learned how to fill it to its maximum. Each time I pack I go through a process of elimination, of discerning what is really necessary. (It is amazing what we can live without when we are bent on the pilgrimage!) I have often envied fellow travelers, especially in India, who are content with a small bag and the scantiest of provisions. Their hands are freer, for assisting, for reaching out to greet and to embrace.

In 1876, three young women traveled from Germany to the United States. They carried little with them. They were emigrants like thousands of others who sought new beginnings. These three visionaries left home and country and whatever future these could offer to follow a dream, a dream of a religious community serving the new immigrant population. In spite of formidable obstacles, they built, virtually from nothing, a community that now extends across the U.S., to several Latin American countries, to Europe, and to India. We who are their heirs are entrusted with that charism, a pilgrim life with a global vision.

It is abundantly clear that we who call ourselves Christians, and indeed we who call ourselves Franciscans, are not convinced of our pilgrim call. Our buildings, our properties, our storehouses, all convict us. Our message to the world around us is often ambiguous or contradictory. Our churches, with their tax exemptions and frequent appeals for money, are often a scandal to those struggling to pay their rent, and maintain their plumbing and roofing.

Francis of Assisi, for one, feared the day when bricks and mortar would limit the outreach of his followers and incarcerate them. In fact, the Franciscan way was a revolt against the monastic system then, which was highly institutionalized. Francis opened the possibility of living as pilgrims, as hermits, as mendicants. I remember vividly a discussion during a General Assembly in my religious community in the early 1970s when there were still tensions about our garb. In the arguments over the issue of lifestyle and contemporary dress, a reticent delegate from Honduras, usually reluctant to challenge her northern sisters, suddenly spoke: "We are debating whether veils have a sign value. In my world the best use of our veils might well be to make clothing for naked children." Can pilgrims afford to get mired in debates about clothing?

Do we devote too much energy to questions of peripheral possessions? Do we misplace emphasis on retirement provisions, video recording systems, birettas, and veils? I know of an inner-city church that badly needs paint and a more efficient heating system. But other priorities so often crowd out repairs and refurbishings. The homeless are hungry, people are in need of health services, those in jail need tutoring and legal aid. The pilgrimage takes precedence over paint and hardware.

On one occasion, I was an ecumenical guest of an Orthodox church in Yugoslavia. It was the celebration of an ordination, an event that attracted farmers and townspeople. The church grounds were crowded with pre-ordination picnics. The worshippers were shabbily clad, even in their Sunday best. But inside the palace of the bishop, clerics of all sorts were dressing in their golden robes and glittering headpieces. Fine furniture and jewelled cases lined the rooms. As the time of assembly began, a procession of church professionals wound its way through the expectant and passive onlookers. The contrast and the contradictions could not have been stronger. A pilgrim church or a pageant? Companions on the way, or a caste system?

One of the great blessings of a pilgrimage is the exposure to the world one crosses. Earth and sky are experienced first-hand: the elements, the terrain, special features of stream and forest and village. The whole of creation becomes a cathedral for worship. The lessons of life and of faith are mirrored in the seasons, in the simple sprouting of seed, in the busy life of birds, in the glorious exchange practiced by nature's population. The Scriptures are visible; the parables leap into life. Poetry and literature and history are at one's fingertips. One trods the paths of centuries and feels the consequences of decisions and mistakes made long ago. A pilgrim passes through the marketplace, alongside the games of children, near the sights and sounds of laborers and miscreants and the humble poor.

When I was in post-novitiate training, I was discouraged daily by my inability to remain alert during the time of morning meditation. At 5:30 A.M. in a warm, stuffy chapel, what could one do during that half hour of silence but return to the sleep so rudely interrupted at 4:45? Month after month, I worried about the guilt I incurred for so many wasted opportunities for spiritual growth. Then, in the first breaths of Vatican II, we were granted permission to meditate in the garden. What a blessing! To pray and reflect under open skies, amid flowers and city sounds, supported by creation with its mysteries and messages. Free to be a pilgrim in the world to which I belonged!

We have moved far from the natural world in which we live. We have insulated ourselves and cemented our surroundings. Similarly, we have created categories and hardened them into the cement of our religious attitudes: sacred and secular, heaven and earth, supernatural and natural, human and divine. And we have cramped our church life into one side of the list. Church buildings are sacred; parks are secular. Heaven is far beyond; earth is here and now. Liturgical cycles are holy; moon cycles and the seasons are mundane. Grace is supernatural; dreams and intuition are natural. Sunday is for divine worship; weekdays are for human pursuits. Oh, we have improved and we have made integrating efforts. We've demythologized, and we've updated our theology. But subtly and often unknowingly, we still separate our prayer and our religious ministry from news broadcasts, the world of work, and ordinary daily events. Topics for sermons have their parameters, and prayer has its own language. Religious protocol is still defined, ordination is still too often an exclusively male calling, the granting of blessings is still reserved for those with special powers.

Most people who were part of the Vancouver Assembly of the World Council of Churches will remember the tent. The worship tent, with a grass floor and portable chairs, had one side open to the campus and the world outside. A symbol of a pilgrim church, a sign of a people on the move, a place of gathering in the midst of, and intimately part of, the teeming streams of seekers and the curious, of agnostics and believers alike. Open to the cries and the criticisms, the cultures and the crises of our world.

Finally, being a pilgrim church means living with other pilgrims, both companions and strangers. The nomad, the sojourner, is not inclined to ignore those who travel alongside. What pilgrim can excommunicate a fellow traveler? Every traveler represents a potential companion, a possible resource, even a possible threat. Hence the importance of entering into a relationship. What we fear most, Geoffrey Moorhouse wrote in his account of a Sahara crossing, is the stranger.[3] Until we have entered that other's world, learned his or her need, intention, and quest, we remain a trifle suspicious. Until we have crossed over into the other's world of images, historical conditioning, and sacred beliefs, we do not have the benefit of exchange. Significantly, Britain has dubbed its ecumenical process, "Not Strangers, but Pilgrims." When we remove our masks, lower our defenses, the gifts of our traditions and our denominations can be freely shared and we can be mutually enriched. The pilgrims en route to Emmaus progressed from tentative conversation with the stranger to a common meal and a transforming realization of their connectedness.

Oscar Romero, of San Salvador, was a pilgrim. He could have remained aloof in his bishop's miter and his episcopal residence. He could have related to his people and their plight as experts sometimes relate to demographic and environmental data. He could have done what all too many prelates have done, divorce himself from the real struggles, exempt himself from the process of conversion and commitment. Rather, Bishop Romero saw the *campesinos* and the landowners, the political victims and the soldiers, as fellow pilgrims. He appealed to the best in all of them, placed himself among them as one of them. "We cannot segregate God's word from the historical reality in which it is proclaimed.... It is God's word because it enlightens, contrasts, repudiates, praises, what is going on today in this society."[4] In so doing and speaking, he joined the pilgrim band of peacemakers and reconcilers, of witnesses and martyrs. He joined the awesome roster of pilgrim saints.

Tragically, too many people associated with the church distance themselves from the very people to whom they expect to minister. What about those places in the world where entering the ministry is still viewed as a status symbol and where church positions mean the assurance of a secure life, a fat salary, and a respected career? It is a hopeful sign that there are more and more clergy speaking out against racism, bishops writing pastorals on economics, dioceses examining their own hiring practices and systems of due process, and religious communities refusing to invest in companies with doubtful records. Yet, far too numerous still are the institutions on the fringes of town, walled in and protected, that reflect "clubhouse" mentalities of clergy and laity alike. We are still reluctant to discard our titles and join the ranks.

The contemporary church in South Africa invites us to a pilgrimage. Many youth have already enlisted and are integrated into the struggle against apartheid. Singing and dancing, miners and mourners are heading the marchers. Men and women, ordained and lay, risk the dangers of prison and punishment while they experience the fruits of redemption and transformation. Across continents and all dividing differences, Christians are challenged to denounce apartheid and yearn in unison for a world free of alienation and segregation. Becoming a pilgrim stretches one's outreach into the future and even into eternity.

We are not yet a pilgrim people! Somewhere in our psyches, we are confused. We want to embrace the pilgrim life. But we also need the permanency of our institutions, our common-sense plans for the future, the dignity and respect that come with degrees and ecclesiastical recognition. We would like to opt for the poor, and be biased in the manner of the Old Testament prophets. But isn't it equally meritorious to cultivate wealthy benefactors and heighten our ability to offer resources to the poor? After all, our church buildings, our palatial compounds, our gold candlesticks and brocaded vestments, do not belong to us. We don't attend expensive conferences, make retreats in luxurious surroundings, or travel by jet for our own private purposes.

To whom do our institutions and possessions belong? Are our churches open and available as centers of community life and activity? Are our cathedrals ecumenical? Do other pilgrims feel welcome to join us in our religious communities for prayer, rest, and hospitality? Why do we hold our theological meetings, and our seminars on justice and peace, in well-rated hotels? Where are the camps and tents and rucksacks that identify a pilgrim people?

A pilgrim existence requires that we extricate ourselves from all that makes us narrow and parochial, that we loosen our definitions of church membership, that we bury once and for all those fossils of our past that are barriers to our common humanity. Can we put off our distinctive robes, set aside our private jargons, and transcend the limits of our denominational and national upbringings? Can we appreciate a worship service far different from our accustomed rites? Can we suspend judgment and easy labeling and walk a piece of the road with the newcomer in our midst? Can we open our minds and hearts to ideas that stretch us and demand a review of our own patterns of living and thinking? "If today the Christian churches are unable to nourish [people] with the bread of life, it is because the church very early on sold itself to rigid conceptualization . . . reducing everything in heaven and on earth to its own dismally parochial boundaries."[5] We are the product and the manifestation of that parochialism.

Two questions in particular arise as I reread the words of *Lumen Gentium:* "However until there be realized a new heaven and a new earth in which justice dwells, the pilgrim church, in its sacraments and institutions . . . ." What are the sacraments of a pilgrim church? What would these institutions be, which "serve the needs of this present age"?

Sacraments that support and enable pilgrims on their journey are surely accessible where pilgrims are. Surely they are administered by, and celebrated in the company of, other pilgrims. Sacraments of blessing and of sending are essential. A sacrament of nourishment. Pilgrim bread for pilgrim people. The sacrament of encounter and exchange.

Must these inward signs of inward transformation not represent the wholeness of life: the overlapping, interconnected points of time and eternity, of human history, and the redeeming influence of the Spirit, of pain and praise, of the oneness of

creation, from the depths of human longing to the tiniest frag-
ment of humble truth? In a pilgrim church, are there different
sacraments for different kinds of journeys: the journey inward
to personal wholeness, journeys of reconciliation and reunion,
journeys toward freedom, journeys of conversion and repentance, journeys of discovery and breakthrough? Surely these
sacraments, whatever they are, are for *all* pilgrims, young and
old, rich and poor, men and women, far and near. The only
qualification to be met is that one be a pilgrim. Can our own
experiences of journeying help us to describe what these sacraments might be?

And what are the structures, the institutions, that are com-
patible with a pilgrim church? The rules and regulations will
be minimal. The structures will be flexible and open to constant re-evaluation and renewal. They will be community-
oriented, shaped, and reshaped by those who use them. Must
there not be structures that aid remembering, that facilitate celebrating, structures for discerning, for communicating, for
healing and pastoring, for guiding and envisioning the path
ahead?

In Guelph, Ontario, this past year, a companion and I made
an ecumenical map. We were there to learn how the Christians
of Guelph understood their mission. We were two newcomers.
"Where would we find the church in Guelph?" we asked. We
were first handed a sheet from the phone directory, a list of the
forty-seven or so churches. There were also church institutions, hospitals, a university, and homes for the elderly. But after our three weeks in Guelph, I daresay we found the church
most like the church of Jesus Christ in a small storefront building near the railroad station. There, a group of volunteer Christians, under the unassuming leadership of a frail Roman Catholic nun, were pilgrimming with the Guelph marginalized.
They offered inexpensive nutritious food, a warm welcoming
refuge, counseling, and emergency assistance. Those who
shared tea and talk with Guelph's poor knew something about
the sacraments of a pilgrim church. Those who bonded themselves across denominations, races, and economic back-

grounds to ensure the survival and direction of this "hospice," knew something about institutions in a pilgrim church. That tiny drop-in center is a flame of hope that, in many Guelphs around the world, the pilgrim church survives.

What Do You Want Me to Do for You?

While we were away recently, a mobile home was deposited just opposite our patio at the entrance to a farmer's field. For some days it was a mystery. Who had brought it? Why? Why here? It was a scruffy-looking temporary residence and quite useless where it stood, without access to electricity or sanitation facilities. (Not to mention that it was trespassing on private property.) Neighbors joined us in speculating about the intentions of those who had towed it here. A few days later, a woman appeared, in a small truck, with six ragged children in tow. One child was barefoot and clad only in a sweater on this cold November day. The mother was hoping to find a parking place for the home and to winter there with her children. That stirred us all to even deeper reflection. What were our responsibilities to this stranger and her vulnerable family? What might the response of a Christian community be to this dilemma and potential crisis?

Jesus said on one occasion to a young scribe, "The foxes have lairs, the birds in the sky have nests, but the Son of Man has nowhere to lay his head" (Matthew 8:20). When Jesus discussed Matthew's future with him over a meal, the Pharisees complained, "Why do you eat with tax collectors and those who disregard the law?" (Matthew 9:11). When a notorious woman burst in on a party at which Jesus was the guest, Jesus reprimanded his host, not the intruder. Was Jesus offering a *modus vivendi* for his followers in these and other encounters? When he accepted a night's hospitality from Zacchaeus, when he ate with the travelers to Emmaus, when he plucked grain from the field for his hungry disciples, was Jesus dropping hints for his own community? Most pointedly, when he washed his friends' feet. (Peter, we know, had difficulty with that.) Jesus said, "It was I who was hungry, thirsty, a stranger, naked... (Matthew 24:35f). Did you recognize me? It was I who said clearly when I invited you to join me, and when I sent you forth on your mission: 'The one who welcomes you welcomes me, and the one who welcomes me, welcomes the one who sent me'" (Matthew 10:40).

Hospitality was a lesson that Jesus never ceased to teach. Whether it was a cup of cold water, a pat on the head of a little child, concern for a sick mother-in-law, or a reminder to jubilant parents to feed their recovered twelve-year-old, Jesus spoke the language of hospitality and practiced it unstintingly. "There is no need for them to disperse. Give them something to eat yourselves" (Matthew 14:16). "Go in peace and be free of this illness" (Mark 5:34). "What do you want me to do for you?" (Luke 18:40).

"Wherever he put in an appearance . . . they laid the sick in the marketplace and begged him to let them touch just the tassle of his cloak. All who touched him got well" (Mark 6:56). It was different from the pressing crowd that accompanies our contemporary superstars. The rock star or the athlete is really not one of us and never asks, "What do you want me to do for you?" It was different from the hoopla that surrounds the visit of a political or religious figure. That visiting prelate or president is really not one of us and rarely asks, What do you want me to do for you? In Jesus' case, the people cried out, "A great prophet has arisen among us! God has visited the people" (Luke 7:16).

"What do you want me to do for you?" When these are the first words on the lips of Jesus' disciples, when this is the signature tune of Jesus' church, then the world will know that the church truly follows its master and that the welcome is God's own. When the Christian community is a hospice for those who are lost and in need of a resting place, a caravanserai for pilgrims. When the church is a place of hospitality, of nourishment and refreshment. When we as church tirelessly tend the wounds, heal the cancers and divisions of our society; when we as disciples recognize beneath the mud and tears the face of Jesus—then the word will go forth and the crowds will gather and say, "You are one of us. You have embraced our concerns and our frail condition. God, in you, has visited this people."

We all know horror stories about the failures of the church to reach out in compassion and understanding. Yet most of us would not say that our churches, as we currently experience them, are inhospitable. On the contrary, some of them are more conscious now than ever of their responsibility to be ecumenical, open to non-members, gracious in exchanging certain gifts and resources, careful not to offend other traditions, and not to make judgments about others' practices and beliefs. There is a greater attentiveness to "building community." There is a growing concern for those less fortunate who are outside the membership list. We try to be more alert to the sick and troubled in our midst, more adept at greeting newcomers, more alive to the value of sociability and of communal celebrations. I was in a church recently where everyone wore a name tag each Sunday. Mine read, Visitor. (Very frankly, I felt less welcome and less included with that anonymous, yet conspicuous, label.)

The challenge facing us is to enlarge our notion of hospitality. To go beyond the traditional customs practiced by our churches on Sunday morning and during the Week of Prayer for Christian Unity. To become a hospitable community seven days a week and in our ordinary everyday settings. To break through the limits we have placed on our perceptions of inclusiveness, whether they be gender limits, class limits, denominational limits, membership limits, to a new experience of Christian community, without boundaries and without narrow definitions.

How will we prepare for that challenge? What will assist us? I propose that the first prerequisite is humility. I am aware that humility conjures up strange ideas to Christians in our day. Influenced by our history, some of us fear its implications, passivity, abasement, tolerance of others' interference and domination. (Women, for example, have been humble that way far too long.) Or, it means a kind of bending backwards to accommodate and please, a weak surrender of one's own rights. A certain spirituality we inherited conveyed that understanding and also impaired our search for truth and for the healthy fruits of conflict.

But our notions of humility also need attention. *Humus* is earth, and we are all creatures of the earth, inextricably implicated in our human and earthly condition. Humility means that we embrace that. We accept our common status. We are one with those around us. Each of us has dignity and also shadows. If we are humble, we can find our way in the halls of the mighty or the hovels of the lowly. We can meet others on holy ground, as co-seekers, as co-creators. Jesus did not abase himself; he ministered. The wellspring of his kindness overflowed into all whom he met, even when his kindness was edged with painful truth.

That is no small task. How many of us are natural, let alone honest, in the presence of a prominent person? How many of us are able to pass beyond the barriers of protocol to an authentic exchange? Do we view as worthy of esteem those who are different from us, those who behave strangely, or look less than respectable? Are we at home in surroundings foreign to us, in minority situations, among those who are ultraconservative, ultraevangelical, of different sexual preference, or potentially embarrassing?

In leading an ecumenical retreat, a colleague and I planned to refrain from programming any Eucharistic celebration, except for an agape. We had had too many experiences of dividednesss at the very moment of bread-breaking, with the resultant dilemmas and pain. We would pray together and celebrate in ways that would reinforce our unity. Since the retreat was midweek, Monday to Friday, there should have been no real obstacle to our plan. Several Roman Catholics present, however, did want a Eucharist and proceeded to arrange one with a priest who was also in attendance. Before we were quite aware of it, the event was announced as well as the necessary exclusion from the communion table of the other denominational groups. Now what? As leaders, we decided not to divide ourselves at the Eucharist and therefore not to attend. Most of the group did participate, however limitedly. Some Roman Catholics were even moved to fast at the moment of distribution, in solidarity with those excluded. It was a breakthrough experience for a number of participants, when after the fact, we shared our individual dilemmas and reflected together, honestly and humbly, on what had taken place.

The event spoke to me of a fundamental humility we must attain in this ecumenical search and in our search to be a hospitable Christian community. We must let go of some of our "goodies," our priorities, our needs. We must stand as much as possible in others' shoes: the excluded, the newcomer, the non-member, the marginalized. We must discern the approach that will gather us into a common connectedness rather than highlight our differences and deepen our separations. That approach will differ in different circumstances. I am convinced that on that occasion of our retreat, we Roman Catholics should have agreed, humbly and together, to fast from a Eucharistic celebration. I am convinced that fasting is an appropriate response and choice when food is not available for everyone or when available food is not distributed to all. I am convinced that in the matter of intercommunion, discipleship is far more important than discipline.

We have to discern as well how to bridge our economic gaps, as in the instance of respectable villagers faced with a transient and perhaps unlawful family. How to assist the mighty in our church structures to become lowly and to empower the lowly to trust in their own priesthood. How to introduce ourselves to our distant neighbors in Asia or South America and to invite their contributions on our common journey in obedience. How to diminish the barriers our histories have erected, disarm the defenses we have built, dismantle the protective rules and rituals that incarcerate us in our parochial pigeonholes. The difficulty, I read somewhere, is not that we are local (or male, or rich, or any other partial category), but that we don't believe we have a link to the global, that we are interconnected. Humility keeps us in touch with our interconnectedness. Pride isolates us, superiorizes us, hierarchizes us.

Humility also enables us to acknowledge our need for hospitality. Who among us is not at some time broken, weary, discouraged, lost, in need of forgiveness? We become communities and persons of hospitality as we experience the graciousness and goodness of others. It was by experiencing the cancellation of debts that the steward in Jesus' parable was to have learned how to forgive. It was by having someone bend down with water and towel that Jesus' disciples were to learn the importance of footwashing. It was by their participation in the Last Supper that they were to learn the seriousness of the commission: Do this in memory of me.

Are we in our church communities too self-sufficient to be educated in this dimension of discipleship? Are we capaable of meeting every one of our needs, at least the needs we perceive we have, and hence remain isolated in our good fortune? Do we take care of our own, with emphasis on "our own"? Do we even acknowledge the need to pray for "outsiders"? How many of us pray regularly and exclusively for our own church leaders or for our own nation's leaders, without thought of those whom we've excluded? Since I have been ecumenically concerned, I am dismayed each time I hear Roman Catholics pray in the Canon of the Mass for our Holy Father, our bishops, our clergy, as if they were the sole church leaders in our world. Is our reluctance to exchange and cooperate in educational and formation programs a sign of our private wealth and our smugness? Do we make token gestures of hospitality, an occasional lecture on the Reformation or on the sacraments, a yearly collection for mission projects, a periodic guest homilist from a Third World country?

Hospitality comes best in the forms in which people recognize it, not in the forms we choose to give it. Do we minister to the real agonies of people with the easy platitudes of religion? Gandhi once said, "It is good enough to talk of God whilst we are sitting here after a nice breakfast and looking forward to a nicer luncheon, but how am I to talk of God to the millions who have to go without two meals a day? To them God can only appear as bread and butter."[1]

Why are we better at debating than consulting, at proscribing than inquiring, at research than genuine search? Are we even able to admit our doubts to one another: Is there an afterlife, after all? Will our world find its way to sanity? Is a marriage still sacred after repeated violence and betrayals? Do we long, as travelers long for their arrival, as pregnant mothers long for the day of delivery, for the bread that sustains and the Word that guides and judges us? Do we even need God's hospitality, daily Scripture, frequent meditation and prayer, the company of other true disciples? For whom were the words spoken: "Not one of those invited shall taste a morsel of my dinner"? (Luke 14:24).

Jesus did not demand that those seeking hospitality come to him. He met them in their need. He went where he could hear their pleas and see what was lacking in their lives. He offered his help: "What do you want me to do for you?" A friend and I had a very shattering experience one Sunday morning. We made our rainy way, with a goodly number of Christians, to a local church. It was a single-person performance, rife with sexist language. The sermon was a scandal, putting down the laity and exalting the role of ordained priest. Insulted on all sides, we exited at the start of the Creed. What common beliefs did we share, with the celebrant at least? Was not our presence a tacit approval of word and behavior?

Unfortunately our car was blocked on the parking lot and we couldn't escape easily. We had the equivalent of one pound with us. Coffee at the local hotel was sixty pence per cup. Wet and frustrated, we presented ourselves and our need. The hotel waitress was amazingly understanding. She found a way to give us two coffees for the price of one. A parable of hospitality. That day we asked ourselves, "Who was church to the two who sought hospitality?"

A priest told me this summer that there were no complaints or requests from those in his parish who were partners in mixed marriages—ecumenical marriages, that is. They were satisfied that they knew the church's mind and were willing to obey. How many of those couples, I wondered, had any faith that their complaints or requests would be heard? And how many had long since given up seeking any understanding or hospitality from the church? It would be interesting to know more about the background for Paul's explicit inclusion of hospitality as a qualification for a bishop (1 Timothy 3:2; Titus 1:8).

Is the Christian community visible where pain is felt and trials are taking place? Do our churches reach out to youth, much less accompany them in their anguished search for meaning and direction?

Do we wait for young people to come to us so that we can play the counselor role on our terms, so that it is clear that we possess the keys? Christians these days are deep in debate about the status of homosexuals. Once we have imposed a label (homosexual, woman deacon, divorced person, ex-priest), we seem able to legislate their lives. And once legislated, no more worry about treating them as persons with the same mixed credentials we all have: mistaken ideas, past failures, heroic efforts, noble aspirations. Mary Hunt speaks of the proneness of those in authority to use well-defined logic (male-defined as well) in their ethical analysis and judgments. Speaking especially of women, and of lesbian women, she says:

> We need to hear all women's life experiences without sanction....One by one, the many marginalized groups need to be heard on their own terms....Only then can the circles of ethical reflection be expanded to include such persons in the formulation of questions, not simply in being footnotes in the answers.[2]

A first step in hospitality is to include in the discussion those who will be affected by the decisions being made! John Bluck comments, "We might look in the areas that the ecumenical movement has avoided and been discouraged from entering so far. Pastoral ministry . . . is the most conspicuous example."[3] It is precisely the area where people win or lose meaning and value.

Only occasionally do the people on our streets, the homeless, the chemically addicted, the transients, find their way into a church building. But they, and the pregnant teenagers, the battered wives, the unemployed, as well as the ruthless competitors, the unscrupulous, and the over-ambitious, are meeting Christians every day. What do you want me to do for you? Jesus was on his way when he met the funeral cortege and spoke to the bereaved mother. Jesus was on his way when blind Bartimeus called out to him. Jesus was on his way when a woman, oppressed by codes of conduct as well as by her physical condition, reached out to touch his garment. Dives sat at the front door of a Christian household, not on church steps. The dialogue with the repentant thief took place on a public hill, not in the temple. Jesus exchanged hospitality with the Samaritan woman at the village well. The measure of our hospitality is taken as we go on our way, not as we describe it from within our cloistered and "clubhouse" churches.

It is right that churches become sanctuaries for victims of persecution. That Christians become convicts for their refusal to compromise with evil powers. That Christian communities become signs of the reign of God, where there are no paying members, no qualifications of cleanliness or proper theological preparation, no balloting, no restrictions based on confessional grounds, no sign but that of inclusiveness.

I remember vividly a scene from the film, *Places of the Heart.* It was a religious film in the truest sense, incarnating the struggle against poverty, racism, sexism. It was a story of family strength, racial tension, economic injustice, of hope and repentance and conversion. In the final scene, the principal characters are at a church service. The church, in rural southern United States, is still actually segregated. But at the moment of Communion, the scene is transformed, by the imaginative vision of the producer. As the camera follows the passing of the bread, the viewer realizes that all who have been in the struggle are sitting side by side: the one who had been killed, the killer, the one treated unjustly, the perpetrator of the injustice, enemies and allies, side by side, in the new community. No one is beyond redemption. No one is excluded, except those too proud and too self-righteous to seek admission. "It's a long way off, but to get there takes no time and admission is free, if you . . . present yourself with your need only and the simple offering of your faith."[4]

Humility is a pre-condition for living hospitably. "I welcome all the creatures of the world with grace," said Hildegard of Bingen. For we are all strangers and in need of hospitality. "Here we have no lasting city, no permanent position, no guaranteed privilege; we seek a city which is to come" (Hebrews 13:14). At the same time, we can all offer hospitality, to open the doors of our hearts, to welcome others into our lives, to host one another. In that exchange, we experience ourselves at our best, as a community. And we reveal our likeness to God who is both host and guest in each of our lives. God spreads the banquet and God is served as food. God offers the bounty of creation and entrusts us with its stewardship. God gives us gifts in abundance, as the basis for an immense network of exchange among the human family.

It is not incidental that the image of God's reign, of the community of God's people, throughout the Scriptures, is that of the banquet. "On this mountain the Lord of hosts will provide for all peoples, a feast of rich food and choice wines" (Isaiah 25:6). "Many will come from the east and the west and will find a place at the banquet" (Matthew 8:11). "I will not drink this fruit of the vine from now until the day when I drink it new with you in my Father's reign" (Matthew 26:29). For starters, therefore, we can study our own Biblical tradition to enlarge our ideas of hospitality.

The ancient Israelites incorporated hospitality into their legal codes. "When an alien resides with you in your land, do not molest him . . . you shall have the same love for them as for yourself, for you too were once aliens in the land of Egypt" (Leviticus 19: 33-34). They acknowledged their status as pilgrims and stewards, "Everything is from you, and we only give you what we have received. We are only your guests. All this wealth that we have brought together to build you a house comes from you and is entirely yours" (1 Chronicles 29:14-16). Appropriate meditations for conferences of bishops, for congregations, and for each of us, as we discern our response to the worldwide refugee situation. As we assess and review our building programs, our financial priorities, our ecclesiastical lifestyles.

"To his own he came, yet his own did not accept him" (John 1:11). How many Christmases will pass with the same motif, there is still no room in the inn? Last year during the Christmas season I heard a poignant tale from Alaska. The homeless in a large city were taking lights from a Christmas tree in a downtown square and were wrapping them around their bodies under their coats and sitting huddled near the tree. City administrators had the lights strung higher so they couldn't be reached. How many travelers have knocked on our door, and we have found polite and rationalized ways to reject them? The neurotic man or woman who seeks our friendship and who doesn't fit into our already formed and smoothly running cliques. Roman Catholic women who feel forced to assemble as woman-church in the face of their oppression and rejection. Children ill with AIDS, or handicapped by color and history, unwanted and unacceptable. Ill-smelling transients or bag ladies with matted hair, unfit company at our smartly dressed tables.

"This is my body to be given for you. Do this in memory of me." We have in our tradition the sharing of a meal, epitomizing the simplicity and the scope of Jesus' hospitality. A meal is a symbol of hospitality in every culture. But we have lost much of the flavor of a meal in our Eucharists. We don't take time to set the table. We bring in the food without awareness of the family celebration we are preparing. Often our bread is brittle and tasteless. I wonder how much catechesis our Eucharists offer children. Do they sense that they participate in a holy banquet? Does the lackluster nature of our table-setting and our meal-sharing have anything to do with the absence of women in the sanctuary? Isn't it incongruous that the people we most associate with family meal preparation are often barred from the altar at our Eucharists?

A family meal always includes those who are not there. Are we conscious of our links to those who have died, to those who are hungry, to those who are excluded, when we receive the Eucharist? John Poulton writes, "Bread set before us brings the starving into our company. Wine set before us brings the joyless, the sick, and those who are denied the fruit of the earth. Fellowship and peace bring into our company the prisoners and the mentally ill, the refugees and the stateless persons. It is a searching, committing act to be involved in."[5] Not only is our bread-breaking to be a sign of our hospitality in community, but a sign as well of our conversion to a more global commitment. At this meal we recommit ourselves to enabling a more human life for those whose tables are empty and for whom society has no welcome.

"In my Father's house there are many dwelling places . . . I am indeed going to prepare a place for you" (John 14:2-3). Our God is a welcoming, hospitable God, even an undiscerning God.

There is a standing invitation to all and sundry. The door is open. There is no need to RSVP. Even those hired late in the day receive a full day's pay. We easily insist on creating a God who matches a description of ourselves. In our hearts, there is room for only a few. Our inner houses are small. And often our churches are too narrow, the doors too heavy or even locked. We are cautious about qualifications and references. We screen and we select and we exclude and we excommunicate. We prefer propriety and validity. We espouse a system of just wages, but we are not incapable of exploiting cheap labor when it is to our advantage or for "a good cause." We don't know quite what to do with those who sneak in at the last minute and squeak past our well-oiled gates and our carefully scheduled rites of passage. We groan inwardly at the possibility of a God who is even willing to be taken advantage of and to overruled.

We can also learn from the traditions of others, indeed from the graciousness (albeit good business sense) of our local hotels and the generosity of our philanthropists. A Jewish man stands in on the job each Christmas for one of his Christian friends, so that the latter can celebrate the festivities with his family. Would we consider doing that on a Jewish high feast day? A middle-aged couple, not formal churchgoers, opened their home this winter to vagrants. Too risky, we say; no insurance would allow it. In India, visitors are served their meal by the entire family, who then remain standing around the table as a gesture of respect.

While we may see no reason to adopt these practices as such, they point to attitudes of welcome and reverence. Perhaps we in North America could begin to apologize for our inability to speak other languages rather than expect others to understand us. We could begin to acknowledge our visitor status in the land we call "ours." Ironically in this era of Sanctuary convictions and scandalous cuts in public aid, the United States continues to proclaim its spirit of hospitality, "Give me your tired, the poor, your huddled masses yearning to be free....send these, the homeless, tempest-tossed, to me."

Perhaps in our church architecture we could learn something from Africans. Whatever is central is most important in their eyes, not what is upstage or distinctly separated. Might our altars move to the center of our churches? At least in our families and our communities we could recover something of the sense of common ownership instead of our ever-present possessiveness. Could not our institutions and our resources be made more available to those with real need? Surely one of our church scandals is the exclusiveness of our property, from swimming pools to large flowering gardens, to empty rooms, unused furniture, and surplus supplies.

How can we prepare ourselves to live up to the standard of hospitality expressed in the gospel? Only by constantly asking ourselves and one another, for whom does the church exist? For whom does this community exist?

If a stranger entered many of our Western churches on a Sunday morning, the obvious answer would be: For white middle- and upper-class Roman Catholics or Lutherans or Anglicans. The same would be true at many of our midweek gatherings, where we tackle the issues of our schools, our flower shows, our choirs, our maintenance needs. Too many of us, in our private and our church-related lives, behave as if we exist for ourselves. Membership is the more vital issue. Mission is secondary and even peripheral. We put our energies into ensuring our continuance. We even propose structures that will guarantee that the power will fall only into certain carefully chosen hands. "Insofar as it (the church) draws people's attention to itself and aims mainly at the preservation of itself or of Christianity or of civilization . . . it misrepresents Christ, Christ's freedom, and Christ's resurrection." [6]

Our experience in Guelph heightened for us the realization that many churches offer a menu, a select diet. Those who are members buy that diet. Keeping the members content and well-fed is the major ministry of the church officials. Persons who prefer other diets are gently pointed in other directions. The church becomes a kind of club, with its initiation rites, dues, sanctions, activities, and self-pride.

In such a context, what message does the parable of the

Good Samaritan speak? How will it be possible to announce glad tidings to the poor, release to prisoners, and a year of favor for all those outside the pale of the law? "Why do you call me Lord, Lord, and not put into practice what I teach you?" (Luke 6:46). Are we not like the disciples who believed they were members of an inner circle and were assured places of glory? Jesus' question opened their eyes to a much more authentic relationship. Can you be baptized, and offer sacrifice, in the church in which I dwell and minister? If so, you do not exist to be served or even to serve one another, but to give your life in hospitality for the many outside your property lines.

For whom does this church, this community, exist? A second temptation facing all of us is the tendency to hide behind our institutional facades. We can't be hospitable (or ecumenical or global or inclusive) if we can't be flexible, if people are not our first priority. I notice a distinct difference when I visit a small Christian community like St. Ben's in Milwaukee or the farm outside Guelph. People are referred to by their Christian names. Horace is the host of the meal program. Willie and Sandy are nightly volunteers. Maxine and Gary are a regular guest couple. Francois, recently out of prison, is the new member of the farm community. Elizabeth is the nurse who has come to live among the farm residents. The lines between those who offer hospitality and those who receive it are vague and indistinct. In fact, interchangeable. An institution tends to use titles or categories. We have bishops and vicars, directors, and their assistants. There are the maintenance crew, the laity, the staff, and the inmates. Rarely do we confuse the specific roles and lines of authority or participation. Almost never are they interchangeable. It is difficult to practice hospitality to groups with labels. We are givers and receivers all; those are our titles and our roles. Experiences of hospitality will transform us into a community of equals, an inclusive, mutual fellowship of pilgrims and seekers.

Our churches and communities are too often in captivity to the structures and the legalisms that prevent us from loving one another and liberating one another. For that in the end is what hospitality does: it liberates us into the world of mutual exchange, mutual struggle, and mutual redemption. Vincent van Gogh wrote:

> One feels certain barriers, certain gates, certain walls....Do you know what frees one from this captivity? It is every deep, serious affection. Being friends, love, that is what opens the prison by some supreme power, by some magic force...where sympathy is renewed, life is restored.[7]

Ponder for a moment what is most of need of liberation in your community or your church, in your own inner system of beliefs and standards. Not long ago I watched a documentary on AIDS. A young man described with great tenderness the death from AIDS of the man he loved. He was not bitter or self-pitying. His face and his ministry spoke of his commitment to help others understand the disease and its victims. Many times the words "gay community" had passed my lips. I suddenly realized the truth of that juxtaposition. That forty-minute film helped to liberate me to the meaning of community, the meaning of fidelity, and the meaning of love beyond death. May not this be one of the redeeming notes in this horrible tragedy of our times, the AIDS epidemic? In the gracious and Godlike hospitality shown by those who live with and care for AIDS sufferers, we have a glimpse of the hospitality of God's new community. Hospitality breaks through the barriers of prejudice and privilege to reach those for whom the church most really exists: the weak, the marginalized, the forgotten, the burdened, the excluded. Perhaps ironically it is they who will teach us the meaning of hospitality. Perhaps it is they who will reveal to us the gracious and welcoming face of God and prompt us to exclaim, God is visiting this people.

✳ 3 ✳

Serving and Being Served

It happens now and again to novices. I was stacking dishes at one end of the dishwasher. It was a hot July day, and the steamy atmosphere added to our discomfort as we transferred scalded plates and glasses onto trays and carts. Someone next to me came up suddenly from a lower shelf and I bumped her quite sharply. I reached down to rub her black-veiled head and muttered, "So sorry." She rose to full height and I saw to my chagrin that it was my novice mistress. She had slipped in to help at the busiest time in the cleaning-up process. Years later I remember that embarrassing shock because it was such a revelation, the leader as servant. I saw her in a new light.

I accompanied a friend to St. James Church in Piccadilly where she was scheduled to address a group. We were early, and we sat in the front pews getting a feel of this inner-city London church with its varied ministries and outreach. A woman came to join us and a conversation began. Suddenly she cast a startled look at my friend and said, "You must be the speaker!" A bit awkwardly she sidled to a safer part of the church. For some, speakers are still a breed apart, to be approached with caution and reserve.

What a "kingdom moment" it is when those who lead, by virtue of position or ministry, cannot be outwardly distinguished from those who follow! What a perfect predicament when we don't recognize the leader! If anyone had slipped into that upper room where a group of friends were celebrating a farewell meal in honor of their beloved teacher, that person would have been surprised. The one with the towel girt about his waist, on his knees, bending over the feet of the others, that is he. Incredible! Jesus was just that dramatic and just that clear. It was precisely the message he wanted to give. "What I just did was to give you an example, as I have done, so you must do" (John 13:15). It was something Jesus needed to repeat one more time, what the real role of his disciples was to be after he left them. They were to be teachers, healers, preachers, yes; but in the same style in which Jesus taught and healed and preached, as servant, available, identified with those in need, one among the poorest and lowliest. Jesus was a foot-washer and expected his followers to be the same.

In spite of his fame and his following, Jesus could be among the people simply as one of them, a human being open to an encounter, willing to respond to any stranger. The Samaritan woman was shocked when he knew more than an ordinary stranger should. The woman taken in adultery expected that Jesus would behave like the other defenders of the law. Frequently people reacted to Jesus with the question; Who is this man? Why is he so different from others who claim to be priests and prophets? What is it that makes him so approachable, so much like us, yet so mysteriously different? No one, not even the apostles, could believe that the Messiah, the anointed one, would be so undistinguished. Much more gratifying to them to be associated with someone prestigious. How disappointed they must have been when Jesus was content to bless children and to mingle among the dusty, bedraggled crowds, when he insisted on having someone sick or blind or deformed brought near to him, when he was open to every request rather than standing on his dignity and declaring an end to business appointments. What a dilemma for a band of followers who thought they were colleagues of someone important whose fame would rub off on them!

"A dispute arose among them about who should be regarded as the greatest." Jesus said, 'Earthly kings lord it over their people. Yet it cannot be that way with you. Let the greater among you be as the junior, the leader as the servant. I am in your midst as one who serves'" (Luke 22:24-27). That dispute, unfortunately, is still being waged among professed Christians. We have not really taken to heart this particular dimension of Christian discipleship. With good intentions we embrace a life of service and self-giving, but all too often we find ourselves compromising and retaining styles of interaction that more closely resemble those of our secular counterparts. We are prepared to go just so far in humility and in participative practices, to surrender just so much of our claim to special treatment. But we can't be naive or simplistic. After all, clergy, doctors of theology, and those with special functions must maintain a degree of aloofness and of privilege. It is not a personal need; it is for the sake of the office. People would be scandalized if those in authority acted as if they were mere servants. There would be a crisis of faith. People want an elite group of whom they can be proud, who represent them in high places. And so on, through the subtler rationalizations of protecting our select advantages and our preferred positions.

Dare we ask what washing each other's feet might mean, in our contemporary church life, within the Christian communitees that you and I know? Dare we take seriously the principle Jesus laid down on that eventful occasion, that no messenger outranks the one who gave the message? Do we actually welcome the blessings that will be ours if we "put these things into practice"?

I smile when I read Canon Law's description of a "Supreme

Moderator," a title that replaced "Superior General." In my community we simply refer to her as Fran. I smile too when on occasion I find someone who insists that a Ph.D. be placed behind his or her name whenever printed. Are titles and degrees really that important? Your Beatitude, Your Grace, My Lord? Even God can be addressed as simply God. "You must not allow yourselves to be called Rabbi. You are all brothers [and sisters]" (Matthew 23:8). I'd like to start a campaign for addressing all members of the Christian communion, including dignitaries, by their proper, baptismal names: John, Robert, Elizabeth, Rembert. Not respectful enough, some will argue. But titles separate and hierarchize, I insist. It is not respect that seems to be lacking, but partnership, a sense of Christian fellowship and equality. It depends on which model we use: a hierarchical, business model or a participative, communitarian model. Surely bishops long to be known as Peter or George, and surely their names can be spoken with as much personal respect as outdated titles convey. Interesting that the Bishop of Rome is referred to as "the servant of the servants of God." A pretentious title actually. And all our titles, from sister to professor to director, should be earned, not automatic. Shedding our titles may put some of us in the position of the legendary emperor, without clothes. Underneath we are just human beings, with no unusual powers or claims.

We often fuss about garments and protocol, incredible contradictions coming from servants! Brocaded vestments, gold crowns, trailing trains. What did you go out to the desert to see? A man dressed in fine clothes? In Tuzla, Yugoslavia, I sat for an hour in absolute horror among a group of Orthodox clergy preparing for a religious procession. It appeared more like a beauty pageant or a style show than a gathering of pastors and ministers. What did it all mean to the passive parishioners who lined the courtyard and flanked the procession, in their worn black trousers and simple babushkas? Unfortunately, many of them were awed by the rich display. A mystique has developed over the centuries among the older churches, a mystique of jeweled vessels, red satin, ring-kissing, and elevated thrones. What the connection is with the one who rode a donkey into Jerusalem and ate with sinners and publicans is vague and tenuous. But it persists in our Christian circles. All of us are prone at some time or other to relish name-dropping and to enjoy whatever tidbits of public recognition our humble positions might accumulate.

Why do we persist in thinking that the only way to honor people is by creating hierarchies and putting the most important personages at the head? Some among us will attest it is a lonely place indeed. Have you taken note of those embarrassing situations where people leave vacant the seats around the guest of honor, out of a sense of unworthiness perhaps, or a fear of having to converse with someone from another world. I get quite an opposite impression from the gospels. People were always pressing to be near Jesus, unafraid to jostle him in a crowd, seeking his presence, his touch, his company.

And why do we persist in introducing people by listing details of degrees and achievements? Are our main qualifications those that are academic or those measured by worldly standards of success? The servant disciple has a very different set of credentials, one would think, and no need to mention them really. They will speak for themselves if given the chance. I remember when Jean Vanier entered a crowded auditorium, walked to the center of the stage, and spoke to us, wearing a shapeless brown sweater and with no other introduction than his name. His own words convicted him as a friend and disciple of the one who washed feet.

Are we willing to re-evaluate our ceremonial customs and our religious protocol? To surrender the accoutrements of honor and privilege, move from head trips to foot trips,[1] discover the blessings that flow from service and equality and solidarity? It is a lesson that lurks in the parable of the Good Samaritan. It was the point of Jesus' admonitions to Simon and to the Pharisees. It was at the heart of Jesus' confrontation with Pilate. Becoming a servant church means, in William Stringfellow's words, renouncing wealth, success, fame, applause, ambition, avarice, competitive esprit, and the rest of the success

syndrome.[2] It means powerlessness, living without embellish-
ment or pretense, free to be faithful to the gospel, and free
from anxiety about effectiveness or image. It means approaching people and one's own responsibilities as minister, as neighbor, as friend, from alongside or under, rather than from
above. It will not be a programmatic approach. It will eliminate hierarchies. It will affirm that the highest among us is the
one who serves, that greatness and littleness have much in
common.

Becoming a servant church means a constant movement toward the heart of life, that is, a movement toward the periphery of bureaucracy and earthly glory. Jesus was born in a
stable on the fringes of Bethlehem and died on a hillside outside Jerusalem. Jesus' concern was always for those who lived
on the periphery. Rather than distance himself by title or temple, Jesus walked among the outcasts and outsiders as friend
and servant. Some Christians are grasping this anew as they
grapple with the implications of liberation theology, creation-
centered spirituality, and mutuality in mission. "God moves
toward the poor," writes Kosuke Koyama. "God is concerned
about their empty stomachs and cold nights."[3] The best sermon I ever heard preached on the feast of Christ the King con-
trasted the style of Jesus' leadership with that experienced so
frequently in our church and society. Rather than being impelled by ambition, rather than climbing upward, leaving other contestants behind, Jesus reversed it: "When I am lifted up, I
will draw all things to myself" (John 12:32).

Jesus, says Koyama, makes the peripheral central.[4] He challenged the self-aggrandizement and paternalism of religion
and politics and confirmed the mercy and shalom of God.
With his scars he blessed and healed. "If the scars of Jesus are
the fundamental symbol for the church, the church must express the meaning of those scars in the way it exists and acts."[5]
Becoming a servant church means becoming more and more a
church of the poor.

"Service to, and solidarity with, the poor of our city and our
world, are central to our self-perception....We acknowledge

our own poverty, brokenness, sin, and need for healing. We are open to being evangelized by those to whom we minister." Words from a parish mission statement. A parish that knows it is sent in mission as a servant community. Sandra, a single parent with two small boys, living on the edge of poverty, belongs to that community. Each Sunday she joins the upstairs Eucharistic gathering, which includes haves and have-nots, resisters and dropouts. Several nights a week she and her children join the meal line that forms in the basement of this church. Out of need she breaks bread with the depressed and the desperate. Just recently she has begun a Friday night ministry at the meal, welcoming guests, serving refreshments. When our positions in our Christian communities are interchangeable, when we are comfortable serving and being served, when the only distinctions between us are those of our unique gifts, we will begin to give witness to the scars and the healing manner of Jesus. A servant church is not a club. It does not exist for itself, for its exclusive members; it moves to the periphery and embraces the needs of all and sundry.

A friend and I were meeting with an interdenominational group of clergy. The subject was mission, the church for the world. How do the churches in your local setting witness as the one catholic church to all the people in that town or suburb? One pastor was visibly restless and upset. Finally he spoke: "This discussion has nothing to do with my situation. There are five churches in East Troy. We have no problems with one another. We each serve our congregations. In my church we already have three hymn books that we juggle. We have enough to do to keep our own houses in order." The church as a club. But not the kind of community that Jesus initiated. "As you have sent me into the world, I have sent them."

In Guelph we found the servant church at the periphery, the reformatory, the intensive-care unit of the hospital, the downtown drop-in center. At St. Ben's, the servant church is most visible in the nightly "loaves and fishes" event, in its outreach to the adjacent county jail. Will it not always be found at the margins of society, the hospices, the mental wards, the shelters for battered families, the counseling centers for immigrants?

A profound transformation will be necessary if our middle-class Christian communities are to become centers of co-responsibility, models of service and of solidarity with the poor. "The one absolute requirement for genuine renewal in the church has been poverty . . . when people begin really to practice poverty . . . then things begin to change."[6] When lay people and people at the fringes begin to participate actively in the life of the church, priests and bishops are invited to redefine their ministries and to join in the march toward a community committed to the poor. This has been the experience in Brazil and in other Latin countries.

This has been the encouraging word from Medellin, Columbia, and Puebla, Mexico. Communities in Africa and Asia are creating their own versions of base communities. In the United States, groups like Sojourners and the Catholic Workers critique and challenge the status quo. Questions are being raised in England about the church's mission to the disintegrating and declining areas of its cities and about a Christian critique of present political and economic priorities. A growing number of younger men and women from Western backgrounds, are finding their way into new styles of living and sharing and celebrating. This is where hope lies for a recognizable church of Jesus Christ. Perhaps one day Desmond Tutu and Dom Helder Camara will not be exceptions. Perhaps the energies of Italian Waldensians, German peace groups, Korean students, and Brazilian slum priests and nuns will one day converge into a church of the periphery.

Women theologians are continuously voicing the contradictions between hierarchy, elitism, patriarchism and servanthood, equality, and inclusiveness. Becoming a servant church means becoming more and more inclusive. My own Roman Catholic church is a glaring study in the obstacles and impediments to such a conversion. The following example applies just as aptly to some Roman Catholic institutions. An ecumenical group arrived late in the evening at St. George's Monastery in Lovnica, Yugoslavia. The resident sisters had waited, not only to greet us, but to provide us with a welcoming meal. Several priests were also on hand to greet us and to eat with us. Not only did the nuns not share in the festivities, they were not introduced, and we were not allowed to thank them personally. Incredible as it sounds, a young male deacon was our go-between, and even the women in our group were prevented from direct contact with the sisters. I might add that this was no doubt the preference of the sisters. But it was a flagrant example to us of male dominance and female subservience. Throughout that week it was the sisters who served graciously, unstintingly. The males had all the places of honor and full voice, at table, in the church, at the conference. But the smiling service of the sisters remains as a lasting memory of the servant church in Lovnica. How the mighty will have to bow low if foot-washing is to become reality in those male Orthodox circles!

As a frequent visitor to the World Council of Churches in Geneva, I have had unique opportunities to meet staff on all levels, from executives and program directors, to translators, typists, and postal employees. As one approaches the ranks of the former, women are scarce and males loom large. But as one enters the latter's ranks, there are women in abundance. For all the proclamations afloat about participation, solidarity, and human rights, I found strong clues that secretaries and book-keepers felt marginalized and powerless. Who were the servants of WCC as large, important conferences got underway? Who were the servants who undergirded the projects that brought acclaim and applause to executives? Isn't it significant that we describe the professions of typists and receptionists as service professions, while we retain "executive" and "adminis-trative" as descriptive of the so-called higher positions? To make me more skeptical, I found that there are 100 points on the WCC salary scale, ranging from top executives downward to the cleaning staff.

How long will women contribute to unbalanced hierarchical systems by their willing acquiescence as housekeepers, sacri-stans, unpaid volunteers, and caterers? When will the humble, hidden staff member be given a share of the credits and the limelight? When will there be a general seating at our banquet tables and a grand mixing of human representation in our sanctuaries? When will persons in authority grant access to power, persons with privileged education listen to the questions and life experiences of those around them? Lest the reference be overlooked, I quote, "Unless your holiness surpasses that of the scribes and Pharisees, you shall not enter the reign of God" (Matthew 5:20).

Women have an established reputation for being foot-washers. Jesus was accompanied by a faithful band of women assistants: Mary, Joanna, Susanna. Mary turned her shame into service as she embarrassed a group of men by her dramatic and tearful ministry. Women risked being identified and punished as they took their services to the tomb on Easter day. In the early church, women were available for every type of ministry: serving as hostess, as deaconess, as missionary, as co-worker and support team. How often we meet a church leader, a prominent speaker or writer, a famous personality, soon to dis-cover in the wings a faithful servant wife! My mother's life was a silent testimony to the spirituality of servanthood. She was the first to teach me the meaning of *kenosis*, and it was she who ex-pounded by example the Last Judgment passage of Matthew 25, though she would have been unable to define the former or recite the latter.

Undoubtedly, feminist spirituality is an important key to our conversion to a servant church. In a very real way, women in the church and in society, have experiences in common with the poor and the marginalized. Like the Canaanite woman in the gospel, they insist, "Even the dogs eat the leftovers that fall from their masters' tables" (Matthew 15:27). But as women tell their stories, plead their case, and even while they continue to wash one another's feet, those with power in our institutions are being compelled to listen.

Women will go on serving, both quietly and publicly. "Some-times we ooze," a woman minister said to me, "but it is in the midst of human suffering, our own included, that we learn

compassion and understanding." "The secret of my not growing old," said a seventy-nine-year-old woman, "is approaching
each day with gladness that I can still be of service to someone." "I am tired," spoke an Indian sister, "but the sick and
needy are there and must be served." A young woman wrote,
"My parents are finding it difficult to accept that I have broken
with my 'sensible' upbringing and have entered a more radical
life of Christian concern."

There is a story that comes from Asia that conveys both the
cost and the glory of servanthood:

> The master of the garden took bamboo and cut
> down her branches and stripped off her leaves and
> cleaved her in twain and cut out her heart. And lift-
> ing her gently, carried her to where there was a
> spring of fresh, sparkling water in the midst of the
> dry fields. Then putting one end of bamboo in the
> spring and the other end into the water channel in
> the field, the master laid down his beloved bamboo.
> And the spring sang welcome, and the clear water
> raced joyously down the channel of bamboo's torn
> body into the waiting fields. The rice was planted
> and the days went by, and the shoots grew, and the
> harvest came. In that day was bamboo, once so glo-
> rious in stately beauty, yet more glorious in her bro-
> kenness and humility. For in her beauty was life
> abundant but in her brokenness she became a chan-
> nel of abundant life to the surrounding world.

The spirit of servanthood is a spirit of nonviolence, of avail-
ability, of transparency, of openness to exchange. "Though he
was in the form of God, he did not deem equality with God
something to be clung to. Rather, he emptied himself and took
the form of a slave, being born in our likeness" (Philippians 2:
6-7).

In rite and in word, we repeat it often. Every Holy Week we
recall the servant songs. Every Christmas we try to absorb

anew the miracle of God divested, incarnated among the poor, servant of humanity. At every Eucharist we relive the mystery of Jesus' laying down his life for his friends and we find our own servanthood questioned and tested. At our baptisms, our ordinations, our professions of vows, we commit ourselves to ongoing conversion. But in the end we resist the role of servant. Anonymity and the last places do not attract us. Unrecognized labor and behind-the-scenes assistance do not satisfy our egos. We easily confuse God's call with our need to be somebody. We mistake the honor and acclaim of achievement with God's approval of our ministry. We find it difficult to believe that we are to be a community of equals or that a daily witness of nonviolence and compassion is as surely discipleship as is public leadership or priestly ordination. Our conversion to a church of the poor and a church of co-responsibility is slow. We are reluctant to surrender our hard-earned badges and insignia. We keep careful track of our success records and our press accounts. Peter was asked three times: "Do you love me? Then serve those I have given you." We are asked again and again by the anguished, the lonely, by members of our own community, to be foot-washers.

The gospel tells us that the little ones qualify for entrance into God's reign. But we can't quite believe that those who have worked hard in the vineyard all day under burning sun will not receive more than the others. Our standards for measuring Christian ministry are often secular in the extreme. Who you know does matter. Putting your best foot forward is tacitly taught. Competition, backroom conspiracies, and ecclesiastical bartering are acceptable political tactics.

"This is how all will know you for my disciples, your love for one another" (John 13:35). We are not yet a servant church. A controversy wages within the Church of England over the preface to a directory. The debate becomes a scandal when a prominent churchman takes his own life. Authorities in Rome respond to their own prophet-bishops with censure and sanctions. Women expressing their own consciences are threatened with expulsion from their religious orders. The issue of women's ordination divides some churches and is a forbidden subject in Roman Catholic episcopal circles. Those with a homosexual preference, even when they have chosen celibacy, are in danger of a ban from holy orders. Homosexuals generally face discrimination, excommunication, and at best, limited tolerance and support from members of their churches. During a recent visit to the United States, the pope was spared the sight (and the corresponding "risks") of a shelter for the homeless. Those living there were temporarily evacuated to a less conspicuous location. Laity live in frustration while church officials belabor the prerequisites for ecumenical engagement and exchange. Persons of faith and vision are compelled to disobey the laws of the church in order to live their discipleship and respond to the urgings of the Spirit.

Every now and then, however, the church has its feet washed. A liberation theologian turns down the opportunity for further study in Rome and chooses a time of schooling in the slums of Bogota. A group of women remain in patient dialogue and faithful communion with church authorities despite heavy-handed authoritarianism. Seminarians join the striking fisherfolk in South India against the commands of those who will ordain them. A bishop proposes that his colleagues sell their gold crosses and turn over the proceeds to the poor. You and I are brought up short by the gospel responses of people who are not practicing Christians. Like Peter we protest, we are uncomfortable in the face of the truth. The grace of that foot-washing is an ability to hear, perhaps for the first time, "As I have given you an example, so must you do...."

Only when we choose both roles naturally and easily, washing feet and receiving the ministry of others, will we enter the mystery of the Eucharist with the heart and spirit of disciples. Are we not forced to ask why our regular participation in the Eucharist does not result in greater transformation? Greater commitment? Greater risk taking? Week after week and year after year we remain mildly energetic about gospel tasks and gospel agendas. Perhaps we are closed to the potential exchange that the Eucharist offers because we are closed to the preliminary formation in the art of serving. As we are converted and become a servant church, we can expect the power of the Eucharist to be released. Blessed will we be, and blessed will be our world, because we have put it into practice! Because we have made the journey from head-trips to foot-washing!

✳ 4 ✳

Speaking the Word of Life

Prepare ye the way of the Lord! Every Advent season the cry goes forth anew. Isaiah announces, "In the desert prepare the way of the Lord! Make straight in the wasteland a highway for our God!" (Isaiah 40:3). Our hymns and prayers echo: "O come, O come, Emmanuel. . . . Come, Lord Jesus, come!" Our Advent wreaths measure our waiting. Once again the world is pregnant with expectation. Prepare ye the way of the Lord!

Some years ago I read a novel set on Native American soil. It was a tale of two friends who were vision-seeking. Clear the way, they were told, make yourselves and your surroundings ready so that when the vision is granted, you can embody it and be an instrument of its revelation to those around you. Repeatedly, since the message of "hanta yo" took root inside me, I have named certain times and moments as "hanta yo" times. Times to clear the way, remove the debris or obstacles, open the path, make a clearing, and lay the foundations so that something new might be built, an adventure might be launched. In our church year, Advent is "hanta yo" season. The hills are to be brought low, the valleys filled in, a royal highway prepared. Our terrains, as far as our eyes can see, the deserts of Ethiopia, the nuclear-missile bases of Greenham Common, are to be transformed, a way carved out for exiles and resisters to be brought home. Our inner terrain as well is to be reshaped, the hills of our egoism, our prideful ambition, and our church politics are to be leveled. The valleys of our discouragement and half-hearted commitment are to be filled. A way is to be prepared for renewed discipleship.

Through Isaiah's prophetic message (43:19–21), God declares, "See, I am doing something new! In the desert I make a way. I put water for my chosen people to drink, the people whom I formed for myself, that they might announce my praise." John the Baptist takes up the shout, proclaiming the imminence of God's reign, the need for repentance, and the unique power of the one he foretells: "I have baptized you in water; he will baptize you in the Holy Spirit" (Mark 1:8). These are voices in the wilderness. We can grow used to the desert with its sparse water and vegetation, its dust storms and empty wastes. We can come to believe that the current wilderness of hostile forces and preying competitors is the only world available to us. The voices of Advent point to the aridity of our tightly scheduled careers, the deafness of our Christian communities, the barrenness of our materialistic and self-seeking lives. "Lo, I am sending my messenger to prepare the way before me" (Malachi 3:1). Heralds' voices. The new Isaiahs and the new Johns. Into the deserts of England and of America, into the deserts of our declining congregations and our episcopal assemblies. Leonardo Boff and David Jenkins, Jim Wallis and Rembert Weakland, Marjorie McGuire and Thea Bowman, clusters of women re-discovering charisms and building inclusive communities.

We lose our way amid the traffic of national agendas and global tensions. We complicate our lives with polite protocol, ecclesiastical machinery, and indigestible exegesis. Though the Word is near us, on our lips and in our heart, we too often hear only the cacophony of our own debates. Messengers sent by God must pierce the clutter of our analyses, the weight of our stubbornness, and the wall of our insensitivity. We ignore the God-sent prophets, and we stifle our own vocations to be voices in the wilderness. We feebly grope for words of faith and challenge with which to address our secular societies. We offer halting testimony to our doubting, delaying communities of the wonders of God's interaction in human history. We fail to proclaim "what we have heard, what we have seen with our eyes, what we have looked upon and our hands have touched...the word of life" (1 John 1:1).

The good news of the Incarnation is for all times. It is the glad tidings of liberation and healing, of compassion and reconciliation. It is the promise of resurrection: love that endures, hope for all who wait, life in the midst of death. It is good news for the whole of creation, groaning under the heavy sentence we have placed on soil and sea. The Word was made flesh in a human life, in public commitment, in concrete words and deeds. The Word is not a formula, not a quick solution for those who seek personal salvation. It is not an easy remedy for sin, not a palliative for those who would escape the rigors and sense of responsibilities of a Christian life. It is not a claim, clutched by those who count themselves chosen. Not a motto or a standard raised in battle, held over against those who disagree. We are not peddlers of the Word, possessing something others do not own and offering it as wares. The gospel is not something we advertise or flash garishly like a television commercial. The good news of the Word made flesh cannot be boxed or packaged, automatically dispensed, or tuned into on Sunday mornings. We are not postal couriers, delivering something anonymously. We are in on the secret, part of it. We are in fact pregnant with it. We have pledged to put our lives at its disposal. It is the gospel we announce, not our own agendas and priorities, not even our creeds and our commandments.

Jesus' message of re-ordered values and re-focused perceptions comes as good news to both oppressed and oppressor, to both the wealthy and the dispossessed, to both the seeker and the sinner. It is good news in its disturbing aspects: what does it profit you if you gain the whole world and lose your very being? Whoever wants to rank first must serve the needs of all. From the one to whom much is given, much will be expected. And it is good news in its consoling and encouraging reminders: I am with you always. Your faith has saved you. Are you not worth more than many sparrows?

In 1983, I was privileged to be part of a team that went in advance to the site of the Sixth Assembly of the World Council of Churches. Two of us began a prayer cell in a small Presbyterian chapel on the campus of the University of British Columbia in Vancouver. Three times a day we called the surrounding community to prayer. At first, only a few joined us: students, local church people. Then our group enlarged; people came from a variety of Vancouver's congregations and denominations, and eventually staff from Geneva. By the time the Assembly opened, there was an undergirding community at prayer, preparing the way for the official work of delegates from the worldwide church. The two of us who rang St. Andrew's bell for four weeks prior to this global gathering understood that we were heralds. A great event was taking shape. The people of God were assembling from all four corners of the world, to give testimonies of struggle and pain, of God's fidelity, and of human commitment. Christians were singing songs of pilgrimage and reflecting together across all manner of boundaries, on mutual concerns and global responsibilities. Our prayer cell was a small harbinger of universal good news: Jesus Christ was, is, and will be forever the life of the world.

Each morning of our lives Yahweh, gives us a well-trained tongue, that we might speak to the weary a word that will rouse them. Morning after morning Yahweh opens our ears that we may hear the urgent need, the reprimand, the blessing. Each gathering of Christians at worship, in discernment, in intercession, each local church remembering and celebrating, is privileged in the same way. Here and now, in a time of natural disaster, or nuclear arms talks, in a time of crisis in Palestine, in an age of terrorism and faltering economies, of cancer research, and in an AIDS epidemic, Jesus Christ remains the life of the world. We are sent forth to announce the time for plowing and planting. We are to be "clearers of the way": a way of peace and reconciliation between neighbors and nations. A way of justice, with new definitions of security and success. A way of acceptance, so that all prodigals may be welcomed home. A way of transformation, so that the sisters and brothers of prodigals might set out on their journeys of liberation. A way of inclusiveness, with doors and tables open to all who seek. We are to be voices in the wilderness, voices that won't be silenced.

Would-be heralds find their formation guidelines in the themes of Advent, learning to wait in hope, reforming one's life. We offer to "bear" the good news, the way a mother bears a child, waiting upon its unfolding, becoming pregnant with its life and meaning. "I am the servant of the Lord. Let it be done to me as you say." The figure of Mary, pregnant with new life, becomes a model. Mary was carrier of that awesome Word. She kept the experiences of her young life in her heart, knowing their meaning would be revealed.

"Pregnancy is at the core of the Christian message," writes Wendy Wright.[1] Once we have conceived the Word, offered ourselves as its bearers, we become someone whose life is intimately and for all time connected to another life. We wait for that life to grow and to pulse its way into our world. More and more we live the mystery of our enlargement. There is really only one life; we are part of it. There is only one Word and we are entrusted with its delivery. Bringing the Word to birth may demand more of us than we could ever have imagined. A pregnant woman should focus all her concern, her routines, and her priorities, on that new emerging life. Similarly, as Christians bearing the good news, we become the womb through which the Word is born again in our times.

To reform our lives means to purify ourselves so that our whole being is transparent with the good news. In a very real way, an expectant mother dies to her own private needs and desires. "Unless the grain of wheat dies, it remains just a grain of wheat. But if it dies, it produces much fruit" (John 12:24). If our voice is to be one with the voice of the one who sent us, we will have to surrender some of our personal agendas and comforts. We will have to repent, accept *now* as the time of our conversion and our submission.

There was no mistaking Simeon's message to Mary, "You yourself shall be pierced with a sword, so that the thoughts of many hearts may be laid bare" (Luke 2:35). And no wonder that John embraced the discipline of the desert, living on its meager diet and clothed in rough attire. Jesus too dreaded the weight of the message that his passion and death contained. Often he said, to himself and his companions, "My time has not yet come." On that fateful night he said to his disciples, "Tonight your faith in me will be shaken" (Matthew 26:31). And finally he submitted, "The hour has come. I have finished the work you gave me to do. I have passed on the message you entrusted to me. Now it is theirs to deliver" (John 17).

A part of our submission and dying is the silence we must observe before the Word. When I was in training as a novice, our directress used to say, half-seriously, "For the first ten years of your religious life you must be silent and then you can open your mouth, but only to breathe." Only when we have learned the wisdom and fruitfulness of silence, the art of active and creative listening, only when we ourselves have been tested and purged by the Word, can we effectively and authentically speak it to others. It is in silence that the Word takes root and gestates. It is in the silence of our dark nights and in the hiddenness of our spiritual struggles that we are re-formed and made into sacred vessels of the living Word. When we are able to regard with silent awe the wonders that God is working within the whole of creation and of human history, we will discern our unique and particular role in proclaiming the good news.

My ecumenical encounters in recent years have caused me to reflect often on words uttered by our Christian churches.

Some convey good news, to be sure, the prophetic words of church officials in South Africa, the persistently courageous tales of women, the bold words of some American Roman Catholic bishops, the testimonies of base communities and local ecumenical projects, the voices, faithful unto death, of Jerzy Popieluszko, Steve Biko, Marjorie Tuite, Ruby Rhoades. There are heralds among us, preparing the way for those less stalwart, clearing the wilderness of rock and sand, so that the Word may be more fertile.

But so many of our pronouncements, creeds, and commandments are heavy and foreboding, excluding and excommunicating. We behave as if the lines are clearly drawn between those who belong to an inner circle and those who need to be evangelized. We define church membership narrowly and by questionable standards. Our doctrines, important as they are, become infallible weapons, rather than limited expressions of limited understanding. Our commandments detail petty offenses. Our basic rules of life are often expressed negatively. We are prone to speak of human failures and to neglect signs of human potential. We sensationalize bad news, mimicking the public press, rather than circulate what is uplifting and encouraging. Thank God, we have entered the era of ecumenical dialogue, but when will we enter seriously the era of ecumenical community? We gather to pray, and we propel toward God lengthy descriptions of our needs with little attention to the intonations of God's Spirit. We speak the Word in our pulpits, in our classrooms, with so much monotonous pomposity. We are threatened by questions, by new theological insights. We avoid whatever goads us to look more deeply into the premises of our faith. We are often so preoccupied with ourselves, our internal politics, that we forget that we are first and foremost to speak a word of life to our world.

The sheer wordiness of our encyclicals guarantees that they will be overlooked. Our church documents are clothed in such ornate and convoluted language that they are unavailable and irrelevant to those for whom they are intended. Many of our church ministers take refuge behind abstractions and generalities, rather than speak their personal convictions. The quality of our sermonizing is uneven: from appalling carelessness and glib trivializing, to self-proclaiming erudition. "Until we recover theology as the delighted, passionate, imaginative, refreshing, terrifying, intelligent exploration of the inexhaustible God, we have no right to claim the interest or attention of the secular world."[2]

Should we not be greatly embarrassed by our innocuous platitudes and moralisms? Should we not be more careful to guard the Word in silence until we have something insightful to say? Would it not be a profitable discipline to precede any preaching with a time of listening and waiting? How many of our meetings and conferences would be redirected or even canceled if we insisted on rules of silence as well as rules of order? We tend to be articulate in every situation, even in those that should render us speechless. Hospital chaplains are often too quick to speak the patients' feelings and too often too many words are spoken at funerals. Could we not hold our tongues and absorb the sermon already preached by that human life? We are so loathe to assume that the simplest among us—children, the self-educated, strangers—have a word of their own, one worth hearing.

We laity often fail to speak of the new things God is doing in our lives, if indeed we believe God is. What a marvelous reversal of affairs it would be if people harkened to the voices of Christians in times of world crises, for an interpretation of the meaning of events, an oil shortage, a famine, a stock market decline, a labor strike.

Christians are to speak the word of life: incarnation, cross, resurrection. But our message is obscured and garbled unless it is consistent with our total word. St. John of the Cross spoke of the life behind the sermon. We can fake one but not the other. Our biography is our conclusive testimony. "Let the word of Christ, rich as it is, dwell in you....Whatever you do, whether in speech or in action, do it in the name of the Lord Jesus" (Colossians 3:16-17). Behind the prayers we pray, the books we write, behind our dialogues and our documents, is the more conspicuous message of our lives. Our human relationships and our response to daily dilemmas are far better flags of our faith than our religious pronouncements.

It is our living word that convinces. The gospels relate that Jesus' renown spread throughout the countryside because he spoke (and acted) with authority. Authority is one of those words we need to recover: authorship, the ability to engender life. We have stolen authority from ordinary people and conferred it too exclusively on those in official positions. It is debatable not only whether our democracies are governments of the people, but whether the church belongs to the people of God. We have removed the power of the Word from the ordinary Christian and assigned it to those ordained or theologically trained. Within that logic and conditioning, it is difficult for Christians at large to believe that they are heralds of the good news of God's reign.

Personal authority is the possession of everyone who has integrity, whose life and word are one. I hear the message of the Roman Catholic woman, married thirty years to an Anglican, when she speaks of the agony of their dilemma in worshipping together. I heed the message of forgiveness spoken by Gordon Wilson in the aftermath of the Enniskillen bombing as he buried his nurse-daughter. The youngest member of a group discussing spirituality speaks as eloquently as his seniors, for he is living his discipleship in the slums of São Paulo. Words of hope and continued commitment to life have a deep impact when they come from the lips of a woman slowly dying of cancer. We gain a new authority among those who mourn, or suffer mental anguish, or undergo discrimination, when we have walked in a similar dark valley.

There is no comparable authority in political speeches or theological treatises. Yes, the credentials of references and research have their own merit. But the issues of abortion, infertility, and divorce must be approached gently by one who has chosen celibacy. The dispossessed are justly sensitive to the lifestyles of those who talk of a commitment to the poor. "Little children, let us love in deed and in truth, and not merely talk about it" (1 John 3:18). Theologians like Frederick Buechner, Rosemary Haughton, Kosuke Koyama, and Monica Furlong have an authority lacking in authors who steer clear of experience. Jesus said, " Go and report to John what you have seen and heard" (Luke 7:22).

Proclamation is always specific, to people here and now. Hence the importance of going where people are, of meeting them in their own setting, amid their daily occupations, within the context of their own language and customs. "The Word became flesh and made his dwelling among us." Not just a limited appearance, a public demonstration of interest, an official visit, but "dwelling among us," acquainted with our infirmities, crushed for our offenses. Not as an outsider making observations or someone on high issuing orders. We do not carry the gospel to others; we mutually exchange the life that Christ has revealed to us all.

Christians are called to dwell among taxpayers and retired people, single parents, university students, and civil servants, to insert themselves as friends and neighbors. For that is where the search is situated, where the questions are being asked. Questions of life's meaning are more likely to be voiced around a kitchen table or in hospital waiting rooms than in our confessionals or the parlors of our rectories. Not that we have the answers. Possibly we will be converted ourselves by the questions and by the fidelity they embody.

In the end, the credibility of a message is decided by those who see or hear it. Respect for the cultures and customs of others is essential if we are to communicate at all. Our cross-cultural contacts have taught us this, and our interdenominational friendships have affirmed it. But we easily forget. We readily assume that our approach and interpretation are acceptable to others. We need to have the outsider's experience in order to surrender our assumptions and preconceived images. We often do not know each other's heroes or religious maps. Our denominational languages are often limited and even untranslatable. It is difficult for us to admit our own doubts and uncertainties, to acknowledge that our interpretation or expression of the gospel is only partial and inadequate, that we depend on each other to fill in the missing meaning and round out the message. "Every authentic proclamation of the gospel has always a definite indefiniteness about it. The statement that rings with finality is false, it lacks the audacity of truthfulness, which intentionally leaves rough edges."[3] Or, as John Bluck suggests, we need to set the record straight by confessing "that we see ourselves and our churches as only part of God's story, that God's purposes in the *oikoumene* run much wider than our present denominational wisdom, and that we're willing to join a journey of discovery and service that doesn't always have to be on our theological terms."[4]

No longer will a restrictive word from distant Rome curtail the enthusiasm or the vision of a renewed community. Or a rallying word from a remote archbishop stir the dying embers of a faith gone secular. Come and see for yourself, someone who is crying, how we adapt to the priest shortage, how we are nourished by our Bible study group, how we benefit from the exchange in our collegial gatherings. Come and see for yourself the paucity of worshippers in our village churches, the reluctance of youth to take ancient practices seriously, the narrow parochialism of our denominational ghettos. "Thus I came to the exiles and for seven days I sat among them distraught" (Ezechiel 3:15). In Ezechiel's case, the exiles were his own fellow citizens, stubborn and rebellious of heart. Today, we need to sit among the exiles in our families and congregations, among those in our world who have been marginalized and made redundant. We need to sit among them and listen to their word and be converted by their faith and their honest search. We need to ask ourselves, Who is bearing the Word to whom?

The world church is our great teacher. It is amid union struggles in South Africa, land reform issues in Central America, political unrest in Haiti and the Philippines that the Word is sought. It is sought in the prisons of North Carolina and North Ireland, in the refugee camps of Beirut and the Sudan, in the cafeterias of our inner-city schools and the rallying halls of young resisters. "What encourages me," Beyers-Naude says in *Hope for Faith,*

> is the fact that sometimes the most meaningful reve-
> lation...about the Christian church and about Chris-
> tian community comes from the poorest...or comes
> from those who normally never believe themselves
> to have any real message....I need to be constantly
> converted...in true humility to sit at the feet of such
> people and learn and hear."[5]

Ed de la Torre is quoted as saying, "You really need to hear the peasants and farmers telling in their own way the theologi- cal perceptions they are coming to. I cannot go as deep, or speak as clearly as they can. You see, I am an educated cripple. I had seminary training."[6] Many of us, church-bred and church-instructed, are crippled by our limited experience and our exclusive points of view. We are not sufficiently aston- ished by the ability of campesinos and workers to find God in their heartbreak and to create something new out of their di- minished and partially destroyed lives. We do not sufficiently grasp the importance of their theological reflections.

The season of Advent gives us a tremendous sense of expec- tancy, of assurance that something new is afoot. Surrounding events become terribly relevant: Zechariah's muteness, Mary's journey to Elizabeth, the census decree. "This is the time of ful- fillment: the reign of God is at hand" (Mark 1:15). But this ex- citement is not only for Advent. Daily events, the significant and the commonplace, can become moments of *kairos* to those who see with eyes of faith and hear with disciples' ears. They were unlikely events: the phenomenon in the sky, the home- less band taking refuge in a stable, the shepherds keeping watch in the darkness. But they heralded a new moment in hu- man history. Now too there are unlikely events: an intermedi- ate-range nuclear missile agreement, a new initiative for peace in Central America, youthful determination in North Ireland to heal a shattered society, *glasnost* and its reverberations. Hills brought low and valleys filled in by the Band-Aid projects spearheaded by a rock singer. Voices of AIDS sufferers calling us all to solidarity and compassion. Stock market upheavals crying out the fickleness of our gambling and our greed. Unlikely events and unlikely heralds. But if our Christian communities pick up the refrain, we can announce to one another and a skeptical world the new things God is doing in our midst.

The good news will get through, no matter the barriers we erect or the obscurity of our own witness. The Word of God cannot be contained, or held captive, at least not for long. It leaks out. "For just as from the heavens the rain and snow come down and do not return till they have watered the earth, making it fertile and fruitful . . . so shall my word be that goes forth from my mouth. It shall not return to me void, but shall do my will, achieving the end for which I sent it" (Isaiah 55:10-11). Unfit messengers though we may be, we bear that almighty Word. From Mary we learn silence, while we give the Word flesh and allow it to gestate and grow inside us. From John the Baptist we learn to speak boldly and clearly, and to close the gap between our speech and our action. From Jesus we learn the meaning of authority, and the possibilities of new life, once we have learned the language of suffering love.

❊ 5 ❊

Messengers of Reconciliation

Some years ago a friend of mine requested a leave of absence from his religious community. He was an ordained Roman Catholic priest withdrawing from vows, but not the priesthood. He went to live and work in another city. He hoped to continue some of his priestly activities in this new setting. Very soon he learned that he needed the sanction of the local bishop to celebrate the Eucharist. When he visited the bishop to request his "faculties," he was refused on the grounds that he was living alone and working in a secular job. It was another step on my friend's journey away from the active priesthood and into disillusionment about church authority and structures.

Recently a vicar in the Church of England, an acknowledged homosexual, announced to his congregation that he was giving up his ministry. His announcement followed the resolution of the General Synod proclaiming homosexual practice to be immoral. He could either continue his six-year relationship in secret or he could resign. Though he had clearly been effective in his priestly role, he felt his resignation was forced upon him.

Two true stories, of rejection and loss, and with questionable possibilities for real reconciliation. They lead us into knotty issues, the readiness of church leaders and structures to take on the hard tasks of reconciliation, the tension in current understandings of authority and power, the role of the community in healing individual and corporate wounds, and the "disturbance" that is inevitable if reconciliation occurs.

St. Paul says, "God, in Christ, was reconciling the world, not counting our transgressions against us" (2 Corinthians 5:19). The entire mission of Jesus is summarized in the work of reconciliation. Jesus became human to bring the world back into harmony with the Creator, for all times, in every place. Jesus' fidelity calls us to fidelity, to conversion, to a life according to the Spirit. Jesus modeled for us the ways of acceptance, forgiveness, self-sacrifice. His lifestyle and his choices concretized the values of the kingdom. Rather than being seduced by power or by any earthly advantage, he was biased in favor of the disadvantaged. He showed the depths of his reconciling love by placing his own body on the cross of our estrangement. "He reconciled everything, both on earth and in the heavens, making peace through the blood of his cross" (Colossians 1:20).

That message has been entrusted to us, St. Paul says. Jesus' mission is ours. Reconciliation is the work the church has been given to do, bringing all things into unity, healing the wounds of hostility and alienation, closing the frightful gaps between persons and between nations, and in creation itself.

In entrusting human beings with this all-embracing work, God also places heavy demands on them. Those called to public ministry, throughout the Old and New Testaments, were tested and purged: Noah, Abraham and Sarah, Moses, Ruth, Mary, John the Baptist, Paul, and Barnabas. It is not the glamour of their positions that we remember, or the status they achieved, but their advocacy roles, their vocations as mediators and community-builders. No one who is a disciple lives for self alone. The disciple "stands in" for others, tries to understand their pressures and feel their pain. A sincere love for each human being is the foundation for any ministry of reconciliation. I know of no more vivid example than an action I witnessed at the entrance to St. Ben's Meal Hall. On a cold blustery day, an old man came for the evening meal. Tom, a hospitality minister, was at the door to welcome him. With a single, simple movement he embraced the man and unobtrusively used his glove to wipe the slimy stream flowing from the man's nose. "By this will all know that you are my disciples, by your love for one another."

Reconciling love is patient and persevering, for its ministry is daily, routine, never-ending. It is riddled with complications and complexities. It takes an enduring hope to tutor in a drug rehabilitation center, to visit in the county jail, to pray for judges and lawmakers and corporation executives. The disciple comes soon to acknowledge that personal limits and frailty prepare the ground for the forgiveness and acceptance of others.

Reconciliation is a responsibility that we cannot delegate. Each of us is part of a pattern of relationships that demands respect and nonviolence. Our spirit will be tested at critical moments, when the funds for our poverty project are cut, when someone else is awarded the honor we deserve, when we are shunned or rejected. And when we are wearied by the tasks of maintaining an honest, caring community. "While we live we are constantly being delivered to death for Jesus' sake, so that the life of Jesus may be revealed in our mortal flesh" (2 Corinthians 4:11).

The ministry of reconciliation has no defined or definable limits. All of life belongs to God and all brokenness awaits healing: distorted and destructive political systems, damaged personal relationships of all manner and making, our own failed covenants with ourselves and with God. Healing is needed in the caste systems of India, the capitalist systems of the West, the places where patriarchy and militarism stunt life and where people suffer the consequences of greed and oppression. Healing is needed in the delicate systems of renewal and rebirth within our larger sacred community, earth. The wounds of broken-hearted mothers, marginalized Indians, excommunicated mavericks, cry for healing. As do those of isolated and alienated psyches and spirits starved for dignity and affection.

I believe it is true that whatever divides the world divides the church. We too have our caste systems, our imperialist empires, our tyrannies, our battle lines. Within our communities are factions and splinter groups, outcasts, and dictators. We are also guilty of competition, exclusiveness, and arrogant independence. We have exploited other cultures and destroyed self images. We have labeled individuals and groups, placed impossible burdens on the weak, made claims unworthy of our Christian calling. Within our churches, as well as within society's circles, we experience the sad results of dualistic thinking, imprisoning stereotypes, racist and sexist mindsets.

Some of our traditional notions of authority and power are serious obstacles to understanding and healing. If sincere love, patience, and nonviolence are conditions for reconciliation, its actualization requires the ability to listen and the courage to surrender any superior advantage.

Some years ago my brother-in-law died suddenly of a heart attack. He was not a churchgoer, and not a Roman Catholic. But his wife and five children were, and he had faithfully supported them in all their church activities, including a Catholic school education. His eldest son, then twenty two, went to talk to the parish priest and to make funeral arrangements. He was shocked and horrified when the priest told him his father could not be brought into the church building nor buried in the adjacent cemetery. My nephew tried to speak about the day-to-day commitment and virtues of his father. But he received no hearing. The matter was closed. His father was not welcome, even in death, in the territory under that priest's jurisdiction. It represents a conception of power all too common among church functionaries. That priest had undergone years of training not to listen, but to be the sole speaker in matters of governance. Moreover, he fully expected the family to accept his judgment and to continue their parish allegiance as usual. And so the gap widens between the one who is broken and the one with control. My nephew has borne a bitterness ever since that miscarriage of Christian compassion.

Where authority is expressed as "power over" and contains elements of elitism, triumphalism, and arrogance, reconciliation is undermined. For so many years the ecumenical movement has waited upon and wooed the Roman Catholic church to join its ranks officially. Many polite words have been exchanged, many broad intentions and commitments offered. Cooperation has been forthcoming on selected projects and within certain limits. Hopes have been raised again and again: by the decree of Vatican II on ecumenism, by papal visits to church headquarters, by joint working groups, by bilateral and multilateral dialogues. Most recently in England, Cardinal Hume had this to say: "It is now very clear that the Roman Catholic church is committed to this Inter-Church Process. This commitment should be official policy at every level. . . ." [1] His words are welcomed and ecumenists of all denominations are heartened.

But reconciliation does not come, it seems, at that level. Officially the Roman Catholic church is no closer now to partnership in the ecumenical journey. What has really changed in Roman Catholic attitudes toward mixed marriages, intercommunion, recognition of others' ordination? "We still describe the scandal of a broken and divided church, but we've learned to live with it again....All the contradictions that made the ecumenists so determined to find a better way at the beginning of the century are stacked just as high as we approach the end." [2]

We know that much has changed at other levels. Community is being experienced, in shared prayer, shared faith, shared search. For those who do not accept the control and the discipline imposed by their churches, reconciliation has moved into all areas of life and faith. There is no squelching the yearning for ecumenical experimentation, for mutual understanding, for deeper exchange. Men and women in interdenominational marriages are establishing their own support groups, and even developing their own worship life and thereby finding some longed-for reconciliation. Women denied entrance to ministry are slowly forming new circles in which they are honored and appreciated. Married priests, the divorced, homosexuals, and other marginalized groups are doing the same; and they are experiencing some degree of healing. People are disobeying discipline and sharing a common table. Convinced clergy are co-celebrating marriages, ministering to students and retreatants and the dying, regardless of church affiliation.

For people at this level, denominationalism is not the issue. In fact, denominationalism is fast fading as a reality. The problem, to those who seek understanding and the healing of their histories, is the authority and power of those in official positions. Sincere Christians are forced to exile themselves, to disobey, to flaunt proscriptions, in order to practice and share their faith as they feel called to do.

The sacredness and the freedom of the individual conscience were stimuli, after all, for the Reformation. As a protest against arbitrary authority and institutionalism, various denominations adopted more democratic and egalitarian modes of government. It would be interesting to research the record of these groups in contemporary situations that call for reconciliation, the issue of women's rights, for example, or homosexuality.

The Society of Friends, now more than 300 years old, rejects a professional priesthood altogether and affirms the equality of men and women. For Quakers, no statement or doctrine contains the final word; every religious pronouncement is open to critical examination. Individuals have responsibilities in matters of morality, and each Friend is committed to serious discernment and disciplined search. It should not come as a surprise, therefore, that the Quakers have been more ready to recognize the rights and dignity of homosexuals. "Surely it is the nature and quality of a relationship that matters: one must not judge it by its outward appearance but by its inner worth. Homosexual affection can be as selfless as heterosexual affection and therefore we cannot see that it is in some way morally worse."[3]

In *Bias to the Poor*, David Sheppard writes, "The church has a calling to be a meeting place, where different groups, especially those commonly regarded as on the margins of society, can meet each other with equal respect."[4] The tragedy is that so many in our world today do not feel at home in any church. And for a variety of reasons: the overbearing attitudes of church officials, the church's perceived wealth and worldly standards of success, its reluctance to integrate the gifts and insights of the laity, its exclusiveness, its unawareness of its own growing irrelevance. The key to churches regaining their credibility and to a sense of belonging for sincere seekers is increased participation in all areas of church life and the acknowledged interdependence of all who constitute the human family. As David Sheppard says concerning the poor and the marginalized, the church will not feel like home to those who have chosen exile or have had exile imposed on them unless the welcome back is authentic and mutual. The churches must be ready to risk listening to those who are "lapsed" and to be converted by their struggles and visions. Love must tie their hands as it did the hands of their founder.

Just as a narrow view of authority cripples the work of reconciliation, so does too narrow a view of the pain and the alienation dividing a community (or family or nation). Reconciliation between and among rival groups, differing factions, wounded parties, will occur when the good of all takes precedence over one-sided claims. When private agendas are transcended. When opposing forces care for more than their own camps. When a vision is created of a community larger than any offended portion, a community that includes all sides and recognizes their interdependence. Some people will have to venture out of their enclaves, their fortified positions, and become spokespersons and links for this larger community. These go-betweens will then begin to absorb some of the pain and frustration of the individual factions. They will begin to forge a new path of compromise, of mutual understanding, of repentance and forgiveness.

In the time we spent with the churches in Guelph, we quickly identified an issue that threatened to divide and alienate them. It was the matter of a new hospital, to be built and equipped fully by government funds, and to be the symbol of Guelph's finest health care. Both of the existing hospitals, a Roman Catholic institution and a general hospital, were bidding for the rights. Feelings were so strong and so divided that business people and medical personnel could not discuss the issue. Clergy who were otherwise ecumenically minded avoided the issue too. The official church seemed to be silent or speaking only to allies. The stakes were high, and of course there was a power component. History and tradition were important factors in the struggle. And because the community of Guelph could not and would not face and address the dilemma, the province of Ontario was about to decide the issue. What a failure if those who represented the community-at-large, the spiritual leaders of Guelph, could not come forward! To enable the anger and frustration to be voiced. To absorb some of the emotion and to examine its deep roots. To speak a language of reason and reconciliation. To build trust and cooperation. To enable the community in its totality to choose the best possible medical service. One speculates, in this situation, as in so many local tensions, what would happen if a deadly epidemic suddenly struck Guelph? Would differences not melt, or be submerged at least, while all dedicated themselves to meeting the emergency?

On a global scale we recognize repeatedly the need for this sort of transcendence. We expect that church leaders will stand in the midst of calamity and conflict and protect the lives of those affected. Cardinal Sin in the Philippines, Cardinal Obando in Nicaragua, and Archbishop Tutu in South Africa are such leaders. Martin Luther King, Jr., was such a symbol in the

1960s. In some tumultuous parts of the world, monks and women religious attempt to be this bridge. Such is the purpose and vision of communities like Taizé, Corrymeela, and Iona. We need those who see the larger pattern, the long-range implications.

The situation in Ireland is a drastic case of religion distorted into politics. Denominationalism, first interwoven with history, is now the channel of terrorism. The churches, knowingly or unknowingly, have exacerbated the conflict. Though the scandal of this "religious war" has been denounced by many church leaders, they have been ineffective in healing the estrangement. Ireland has been shaped by its memories. In Alan Falconer's words, "History holds a community captive. . . .The memory imprisons."[5] How can the rights of the "other" be restored in Ireland's fragmented self-image? What can reawaken a sense of interdependence, of a common destiny? Who can enlarge Ireland's sense of responsibility to include history's mistakes and today's hostilities? "An ecumenical theology of peace needs to address the hurtful memories, and the root cause of fear in all the communities, namely the way in which power has been exercised and is currently exercised by the 'other' community."[6] Perhaps old wounds need more airing. Perhaps the needs and dreams of the whole population need more articulation. If individuals are not able to lead the way in this process of healing, could small integrated communities shoulder the burden? By listening to one another and learning how each other's fears have been formed, by looking together at a common future, at common hopes? By believing enough in their vocation as church, could such cells be instruments of the Spirit in bringing about a resurrection in Ireland?

Whether the stumbling block is authoritarianism or a myopic view of community, disturbance is inevitable. For there will be no reconciliation without conversion and change. For many people, peace means the absence of conflict, of confrontation. Some settle for an avoidance of contact. Members of families, and of communities are familiar with this route. Its limitations are soon evident. Communication is strained, spontaneity is lost, and eventually trust is so eroded that relationships disintegrate. Avoiding contact or conflict will never remove the haunting summons to confess and convert.

For some, reconciliation means adjustment, a shifting of mental furniture. It means accepting an unfortunate situation, and adapting to whatever interchange remains possible. Reluctantly, two sides agree that neither will change. Implicit in this agreement is each side's conviction that no fault can be laid at "my door." Perhaps the distance can be maintained, but little growth will be possible and the creative will be stifled.

Where reconciliation occurs, repentance leads the way. Nothing equals the power of repentance to break a deadlock. And often nothing requires more courage than admission of fault. The disturbance that repentance evokes in our personal and collective psyches is so jarring that we tend to exhaust every other available dynamic before we succumb. We dread the bald admission of our wrongdoing! We shrink from taking that first step that will inevitably mean disruption and sacrifice. In our personal lives, we fear the loss of control. In our churches, we prefer to pray our repentance or preach it, rather than practice it in relation to the neglected poor, marginalized women, disenfranchised laity. Repentance means humble truth and the truth is costly.

> There has to be a giving out of energy. For the one who makes the first move, there is generally a costly giving away of self. There is then an answering giving out of energy from the other person, in response and change of heart....The streams of energy from both parties come together into a kind of pool of energy.[7]

With this new supply of energy, the broken relationship can possibly be repaired. Once the initial breakthrough is made, a new balance is created. Focus shifts from the offense to the new gift. Faith in the integrity and authenticity of the other returns. Forgiveness may follow.

That is, if stubbornness does not interfere. I daresay that

many of the divisions, on our personal journeys and in the history of Christianity, have been deepened and sustained by mutual and blind stubbornness. Refusals to dismount our self-made thrones, to share our portion of the burden and guilt. Insistence that our pride be assuaged, our complaints appeased. Impasses and silence, self-justification, and rash judgment. Cycles of accusation and of resentment. Until memories are branded with pain and bitterness.

"I am sorry" may be among the most difficult words in our language, but once they have cleared the throat, they have the potential to clear the air of stagnant rancor and to free us from our paralysis. To be effective, however, they must be the first words in a process of restitution and of justice. It is not enough for some church prelate to say to my resigned priest-friend, or the homosexual vicar, "I am sorry." A new pattern must emerge, of listening and dialogue. A new commitment must be evident to build a church big enough to embrace all styles of living and ministering.

A word of comfort means little to the Honduran *campesino* without the pledge of the wealthy landowner to rectify the evils of inequality and greed. No apology will heal the wounds of women deprived and dismissed, without the action of conscientious persons to dismantle oppressive systems and to welcome total participation. What the "sinned against" seek in each case is recognition of their suffering and struggle, a more just distribution of power, and a restored wholeness that fosters belief in the birth of a new community. Those who repent must be willing to cope with the pent-up energies and the creativity that will inevitably well up and disturb the status quo. They must be willing to integrate the new structures, the new roles, the unforeseen costs that will appear once autonomy is surrendered.

Our God is a disturbing God who wrestled with Jacob, who inspired Rahab to civil disobedience, who forced Paul to his knees, and inspired Jeanne d'Arc into battle. This same God probes us in our complacency and comfortability. This same God prods us to risk, to make contact with those whom we have excommunicated, to rebuild the fabric we have torn and the bonds we have broken.

The inability to repent is a refusal of life. Conversely, reconciliation is a renewal of life. It is, in fact, a resurrection. A minor rift between neighbors illustrates this. Ann feels a growing animosity when a nearby homeowner allows smoke to blow on her newly painted cottage, then encroaches on her property to build a driveway. A series of small incidents mount until she is exasperated. Finally, his decision to burn a light that shines into her bedroom window all night brings the tension to open conflict. Then winds of hurricane strength do their own damage while Ann is in another part of the country. Four tiles from her roof are smashed. Her neighbor offers four new tiles of his own and helps repair her roof. That small sign of reconciliation is sufficient. Ann goes to make peace. A new blossom of good will. And the light is put on a timer so that blessed darkness returns to the cottage.

Stories of resurrection in our daily lives. Born out of honest self-revelation and gentle response. So many of the healing stories in the gospels convey this pattern. I am a leper; cure me. I am blind; restore my sight. We are afraid; calm the storm. I am a public sinner; forgive me. New life began in that moment in which each one presented an honest need. "Go in peace" was Jesus' reply.

One of the criminals crucified with Jesus acknowledged his guilt, throwing himself onto Jesus' mercy. The self-absorbed thief, on the other hand, continued cursing and swearing. With his desperately longing words, "We are only paying the price for what we've done, but this man has done nothing wrong," the repentant thief entered the flow of forgiveness and reassurance. "This day you will be with me in paradise."

Peace was Jesus' farewell gift, a peace unlike anything the world knows, because it is always available, always renewable, unqualified and inexhaustible. It is that gift that makes our reconciliations possible. Our own human peace is sporadic and partial, hesitant and measured. But we have access to that gift beyond human expectations. We can draw on it when our own resources fail us.

Peace was also Jesus' resurrection greeting to the first women apostles, to the anxious disciples gathered in a locked room. Through the centuries it has been Christian tradition to mark a reconciliation with the greeting of peace, as sins are forgiven, differences healed, strangers made friends, hearts reunited.

Blindness and fear, complicity with evil, stubbornness, and pride are refusals of life. Peace will not break out in the villages of Ireland, the hinterlands of Central America, the streets of Seoul and Los Angeles until Christians, among others, disarm themselves of prejudice and greed. Life and energy will not be released from within the narrow walls of our churches until all possible borders are crossed (Protestants and Roman Catholics, Orthodox and Jews, clergy and laity, men and women), and gifts are freely exchanged. The symbols, stories, and songs of diverse cultures will not enrich and nourish our communities until we enlarge our vision and build a community as vast as the world. The beauty and fruits of creation will not last to bless our lives unless we repent of our waste and carelessness.

Each life, and each community is as fragile as the shoots of a spring bulb poking its way through the soil into the crisp spring air. Resurrection awaits us whenever we mend an eroded relationship, focus outward, and extend our boundaries. Resurrection awaits us whenever we gather our enemies into our prayer and pluck from our hearts the seeds of superiority and self-sufficiency, offering mercy rather than judgment, a peaceful gesture rather than prolonged silence.

Resurrection awaits also those caught in the gaps of repentance and conversion. "You are a priest according to the order of Melchesidech" (Hebrews 7:17), in spite of the frozen and fixed disciplines of the church. "In my Father's house there are many mansions....I will prepare a place for you," even if you are denied a Christian burial. "I was ill in Guelph's hospital while you were absorbed in your politics and power struggles." Belfast, "if only you had known the path to peace this day; but you have completely lost it from view . . . you failed to recognize the time of your visitation" (Luke 19:42,44). "I tell you all this that in me you may find peace" (John 16:33). Having tasted it and experienced your moment of resurrection, you may become at last my messengers of reconciliation.

✳ 6 ✳

More Than a Story

Bourj al Barajneh is a refugee camp in Beirut. It could be in the Sudan or Honduras or Pakistan, for it mirrors the plight of millions of people without a homeland. Pauline Cutting, a British surgeon, who helped alert the world to the misery inflicted on a group of Palestinians, has written a book, *Children of the Siege*. Horror stories of starvation, fear, despair. And for some, a story of survival. It is particularly a story of victims, caught up in the viciousness of war and the political turmoil that persists in the Middle East. Admitting that her extraordinary experiences have not given her religious faith, Dr. Cutting comments that some of the atrocities are being committed in the name of God.

Often the blame for human suffering is laid on God. Religious divisions, as well as political, are perpetuated in God's name. Both sides engaged in hostilities invoke God's sanction. The consequent suffering is deemed necessary to achieve God's designs. It is an ancient argument, from the Crusades to the Reformation and into our own era, in the Middle East, India, Spain, and Ireland. Repeatedly religions and churches have contributed to the distorted relationship between human suffering and religious rights.

To some extent we are all captives of our cultural backgrounds as we face questions of evil and of suffering. Some of us have been conditioned to interpret personal tragedies and losses as God's punishment. Or to believe that accidents and illnesses are God's will, sent to test us and to toughen us for life's future crises. Even to accept that suffering is a mystery not ever to be questioned. In various ways our religious faith has often reinforced these beliefs. How well I remember instances in my own life when blind obedience, regardless of its doubtful side-effects, was equated with God's will. How many Christians still believe that economic fortune or misfortune is sent by God! That to question God's designs in the death of a loved one, is to blaspheme! That attempting to comprehend the forces of evil and the mystery of human pain is to be arrogant and presumptuous! God, it would seem, has a right to be arbitrary; and humans with faith have no right to doubt God's ways. We have all experienced the pious platitudes of well-meaning pastors and ardent fundamentalists. Currently from the lips of Christians we hear blatant judgments of AIDS sufferers, alcoholics, battered women. "They brought it on themselves." "They are being punished for the way they have lived." God, for many people, is still an avenging God, a heartless judge, one who tests and measures the human spirit.

We may well ask, what kind of world is it (not what kind of God) that permits the suffering and terrorizing of so many innocent human beings? How can religious people manipulate and distort their beliefs to justify brutality and injustice? How do those who profess belief in a creative and loving God account for the misery and madness that fill our television screens and provide our news headlines? Perhaps the question is not, How can God allow the torture and massacre of so many? But rather, How can we allow it, even collaborate with it? How can we stand amid pain and bereavement and content ourselves with packaged explanations and prefabricated allowances for human sin and neglect? What is the creative relationship between our helplessness in the face of human suffering and our faith? "O Lord, our hearts are heavy with the sufferings of the ages, with the crusades and the holocausts of a thousand thousand years....To you we lift our outspread hands. We thirst for you in a thirsty land."[1]

Pauline Cutting went to Beirut as a voluntary and anonymous health worker. The visible suffering of her fellow human beings transformed her into their spokesperson, into someone who shared their hunger and their fear of death. The Pauline Cuttings of our world (and the Ben Lindners) make the Incarnation something more than a story. The Incarnation is in actual time, amid real people in real situations. The Incarnation is about response to pain and injustice and human frailty. Jesus became as helpless as the Samarian refugees or the Roman captives. He became an advocate for victims of oppression and prejudice. He bore in his own being the marks of physical torture, mental anguish, and spiritual abandonment. He turned helplessness into self-sacrifice. In so doing he proposed an answer to the question, Who is God, who sees the innocent suffer and die?

The God of Jesus is a God who bears the sufferings of human beings, carries their grief, loneliness, despair. A God who bears as well the indifference and cruelty of creatures, their rejection and scorn, their denial and distortion of divine purposes. In the New Testament, images abound of a God whose love is limitless, who suffers with the human family, who makes the cross the sign of divine involvement in every human tragedy. Jesus' God is one who protects even the birds and wild flowers. This God is at least as good and as generous as the best of human parents. This God identifies with everyone who is hungry, thirsty, naked, homeless, ill, or imprisoned. This God's mercy and compassion transcend human laws, codes, judgments. This God is a shepherd, forgiving father, servant, and, above all, active love. This God is in fact the reverse of all that people might expect God to be. "Has not God turned the wisdom of this world into folly?" (1 Corinthians 1:18). God's weakness and vulnerability, which lavishes unconditional love on the most unworthy, is more powerful than any human strength, even that bent on persecuting and crucifying.

> Therefore He who Thee reveals
> Hangs, O Father, on that tree
> Helpless; and the nails and thorns
> Tell of what Thy love must be.
> Thou art God; no monarch Thou
> Thron'd in easy state to reign;
> Thou art God, whose arms of love
> Aching, spent, the world sustain.[2]

Our response to suffering, our own and others', reveals our comprehension of God. Like Pauline Cutting, we may not articulate that understanding in religious language. But how we relate to the agonies of our world indicates our underlying assumptions about God's relationship to the human family and about our bonds with one another. Confronted with the threat of nuclear war, the evils of racism, the miseries of poverty, the ravages of cancer, we choose either moral insensitivity and passive acceptance, or peacemaking efforts and deeds of love and mercy. God does not control the policies and structures that create or prolong human suffering. "God is not accountable to us for the senseless harm we cause one another. We are accountable to God."[3] God rules the world through us, instruments of justice or repression, instigators of freedom or fear. The Christian community, the church, exists to remind each age of that choice and that responsibility. But the church must constantly remind itself of the divine trust placed in human hearts and minds. "We have lived so long," says Walter Bruggemann, "in this competitive, adversarial place, that we have come to think it is where we belong....We are children of the language of the Cold War, of the rhetoric of competition and the ideology of individualism, of the practice of fear and hate and greed."[4] As believers in God's reign, we bear the awesome sense of responsibility of viewing and organizing the world differently. Of being agents, both actively and subversively, of a society that regards human life with reverence and works to reduce human degradation.

We are not to deny the reality of suffering or to spiritualize it out of existence. We cannot bypass life's evils and struggles, and take comfort in a distant heaven. We are people of the Incarnation. Our faith is manifested in everyday encounters with consumerism, militarism, and the many seductions of our twentieth century. Nor are we to endorse suffering for its own sake. Some of our traditions have given support to a cult of suffering that condones everything from self-pity and self-inflicted mortification to self-imposed martyrdom. Rather, our Christian vocation calls us to distinguish between redemptive pain and unnecessary affliction. The cross is a condition for discipleship. Jesus shared fully in our humanity. "Since he was himself tested through what he suffered, he is able to help those who are tempted" (Hebrews 2:18). In God's order of things, we do not choose our own crosses, nor do we set out to provide crosses for others to carry. Our very humanness suffices to guarantee suffering. At the same time we must make every effort to eliminate and alleviate pain and what causes it. A task of the Christian community is to discern, to give counsel, to show leadership.

Bearing the crosses that come into our lives is as important as guarding against those that are unnecessary. At whatever level suffering strikes, it can be a means of our diminishment or a means of our growth and liberation. Some are broken by their crosses and live bitter lives, unredeemed by new insights and deeper sensitivities. Others find their way through suffering to greater strength and a wider reservoir of peace and wholeness. Suffering seems to release a radiance in some people, and the spirit communicates even when the body is trapped in physical limitations. The history of many individuals and peoples reveals how suffering enhances creativity and increases an energy for greater life. Similarly, those who help bear the burdens of others find their lives expanded and enriched. Pain changes our perspective. It jostles all that seemed fixed and permanent. "Through joy," says Simone Weil, "the beauty of the world penetrates our soul. Through suffering it penetrates our body."[5]

Suffering identifies who we really are as a Christian community and as individual believers. "You will suffer in the world," Jesus spoke plainly. "But take courage, I have overcome the world" (John 16:3). Throughout history and today as well, the body of Christ undergoes oppression and repression, from the misguided and the malicious. Tremendous fruit is borne from the witness of martyrs. It is a fact that the church is most alive and vibrant where it suffers most. Luther once named suffering as one of the marks of the true church. "We are called to be a confessing church. . . . Martyrdom is a daily affair for Christians. However faithless the church has been . . . in risking all and following the way of the cross, it has also borne the marks of the passion in countless of its members." [6]

Suffering also uncovers the depths of personal faith. "We experience victory over suffering when we receive it and absorb it and make it contribute powerfully to who we are."[7] In our moments of personal crisis, we look toward those who have journeyed before us through difficult terrain. "You shall be pierced with a sword, so that the thoughts of many hearts may be laid bare" (Luke 2:35). Perhaps the most inspiring moments of a recent women's retreat were those we spent storytelling: bereavements, worries, anguish, physical afflictions. In the solidarity of our tears, our treasured memories, and our trials endured, our faith was nourished, and our solitary journeys took on new meaning. Suffering entered into and overcome is a parable from which others learn and are empowered.

Cruelty and suffering have become so familiar to us, albeit in the safe comfort of our television lounges, that our very ability to empathize is threatened. The media, in multiple forms, are such a prominent feature of daily life that it seems obvious that their influence must be a regular part of our Christian review and reflection. In the Western world especially, the churches have a rare opportunity to provide a new structure of spiritual renewal, monitoring and critiquing daily news and what passes as entertainment. Television has the potential for creating a global community. But its frightful challenge is its indiscriminateness. We are numbed by its unfiltered barrage of violence, sadism, triviality, and variety of information. Our sense of proportion is constantly under attack. In one instant we are in Ethiopia with starving refugees and in another we are mindless spectators of a cat food commercial.

How does faith address the choices and the effects of television viewing? As members of a Christian community, how do we assist one another, and especially our children, in developing skills of criticism, connection making, and the ability to remain vulnerable to human suffering? Television is an ecumenical issue in its ambiguities, and in the resource it offers for our sermons, retreats, intercessions.

"The true perspective of our lives," writes J.V. Taylor, "is not the small, moderate bourgeois world that we pretend is ours but a cosmic struggle on which the great extremes of the Gospel are stark realities—light and darkness, life and death, luxury and starvation, heaven and perdition."[8] For some of us, television brings this cosmic struggle into focus. Our narrow worlds of work and home, petty quarrels and persistent problems, are enlarged and unlocked by our contact with distant places and peoples. For others, these "great extremes" are first-hand experiences—unemployment, homelessness, hunger, disease. But these worlds apart are far more related than most of us realize. We are all interconnected in a vast pattern of light and darkness, life and death. Through television we are implicated in each others' lives and in each others' sufferings.

The suffering of any one people has international roots. The suffering of any one person has far-flung effects. "There is no pain or passion that does not radiate to the ends of the earth."[9] The peasant alienated from the land and the worker alienated from the product are part of a pattern that has put food on others' tables and conveniences in their homes. An unemployed youth bears the seeds of bitterness that will pollute friends, family, and even future generations. Political prisoners, of whatever persuasion, have a common yearning for freedom. Exile, isolation, and bereavement have multiple forms. In the perspective of the Gospel, we are all diminished by the suffering of any part of the body. We are restored and healed to the degree that our subjective suffering is part of a vast movement toward wholeness and to the degree that we become surrogates for the sufferings of others. The cure for suffering is a greater kind of suffering.[10]

There is no denying that suffering is particular and that each of us hangs alone on our cross. "Pain is the most individualizing thing on earth," Elizabeth Hamilton has written. "To suffer is to be alone. To watch another suffer is to know the barrier that shuts each of us away by ourselves." "At the same time, that which isolates us binds us. How many parents have passed through Lindberghs' "hour of lead"? How many victims of war and terrorism have felt the agony of suspense and terror as they awaited word of loved ones? How many grieving mothers have stood with the *Madres de Mayo* in Argentina? How many of us know the "waiting room anxiety," outside surgery, after an accident, following a job interview?

What does all this mean for our search for an ecumenical spirituality? It means, first of all, that the ministry of suffering may be more important than the ministry of words. Jesus summed up his teaching about detachment and penance in his silent march to Golgotha. His words became effective in his submission to nails and insults. A Methodist minister dying of cancer may be offering his congregation something more precious than his years of faithful pastoral ministry. Corazon Aquino's reported surrender of family property to the general policies of agrarian reform may be among her noblest decisions. I remember a Bible study in an ecumenical setting. We were reflecting on Ephesians 6, "Our battle is not with human forces but against the principalities and powers, the rulers of this world of darkness." One by one we became mute as our

Korean brother related his own imprisonment and beatings, his solitary prayer as he awaited the next moment of terror.

Perhaps we must all weigh our words more carefully in the face of the accumulated suffering of our congregations. And think twice before we speak about the cost of divestment or displacement, double-checking that we know whereof we speak. Perhaps we must yield our pulpits and our pens to those among us who have already lifted and drained the cup of suffering.

Secondly, it means that we must examine our church life, our witness, to see if we are a stumbling block rather than a sign of the resurrection. Does our own suffering, and our response to it, testify to the victory of life over death? Do we allow our trials to become an entrance into the trials of others? Is it apparent that in our hollowing out, through setbacks and struggles, we find meaning and become more sensitive? Does our faith shine through?

Or, are we so scarred and defeated that we cannot heal, so burdened that we cannot lift up voices in praise or hands in blessing? Are we merely another social agency, relieving some immediate stresses, offering some temporary solace? Do we seek a refuge from daily problems, soothing ourselves and others with promises of a hereafter, subtly teaching a gospel of success and inevitable progress? Do we suppress legitimate fears and angers, cover up uncomfortable memories or tensions, and limit one another's real expectations? Do we bore some by our shallow, pious solutions, and repel others by the same? Do we cry "Peace, peace," where there is no peace, rather than shoulder the tasks of peacemaking?

The church of Jesus Christ is above all ecumenical in its suffering. It unites the people of Uganda and Guatemala, of Korea and South Africa, of Russia and Pakistan. In every part of the world, the cross is lifted up, the passion is repeated. Christians still take on the roles of Simon the Cyrene, Joseph of Arimathea, Mary Magdalen, and Salome. "Never be ashamed of your testimony, but with the strength which comes from God bear your share of the hardship which the gospel entails" (2 Timothy 1:8).

Each of us is implicated in the poverty of India's *harijans,* the shame of Filipino women, the bleak destinies of countless Asian children. In them we hear the groaning of the hungry, the cry of the voiceless, the anguish of the landless. The awesome endurance of the people of Asia demands from us a new reverence for every form of life.

Each of us is related to the political prisoners of Chile, the endangered coffee-bean growers of Nicaragua, the "disappeared" of Argentina. In them we see "a humble and human God, a God that sweats in the streets, a God of worn and leathery face."[12] The courage of Latin Americans invites us to participate in their common project, their exodus toward a new society.

The shadow of Africa's suffering lengthens across our own spirits. We feel the alienation of South African youth, the desperation of East African refugees, the fatigue and sorrow of Ugandan families. "Oppressed and condemned, he was taken away....he was cut off from the land of the living . . . a man of suffering accustomed to infirmity" (Isaiah 53: 8, 3). The persistence of our African brothers and sisters demands repentance for our own racist inclinations and inspires us to believe in our small efforts to build and restore community.

Our lives and histories are linked with the plight of Amerindians, Aboriginals, Maoris, whose identity has been destroyed and whose lands have been robbed and wasted. "God is the memory that forgets no one."[13] God is the Great Spirit who does not faint nor grow weary, who lifts up the faltering on eagles' wings. These primal peoples hauntingly remind us of our false securities, our short memories, our tragic indifference to land and water and sky.

In our affluent societies, suffering has unique but familiar faces, the pressures of careers, the loneliness of anonymous and mobile lifestyles, the fear of violence, the pain of emptiness. We glimpse a never-dying hunger for something larger and more transcendent. We sense a growing panic that so much having provides so little real peace and inner harmony. The search and yearning of comfortable Western neighbors prompt us to re-assess our treasures, and to live in the consciousness of our mortality.

These global links also reveal the hopes of the whole human race. If the body of Christ were to become aware of its suffering members and unite in an immense outpouring of energy, what redemption might be possible? "All creation groans and is in agony." Suffering cannot and should not separate us from one another. Rather, trial and distress, persecution, hunger, nakedness, danger and the sword, should bind us together in an invincible network of solidarity and strengthen us for our individual and common Gethsemanes.

What if we who call ourselves Christians were to stop quoting the Scriptures and more consciously pray them, the servant songs of Isaiah, the prophecies of Amos, the psalms of the exiles, the farewell words of Jesus? What if we became rooted in the pain of God, pleading with Ephraim, weeping over Jerusalem, until we were moved to offer our bodies at the Nevada test site, the borders of Honduras and Nicaragua, the front lines of every struggle within reach?

What if we who call ourselves Christians were to stop adoring the cross and stoop to lift the burdens of speaking the truth, of social analysis, of political criticism? To acknowledge our complicity with exploitative systems, our unwillingness to divest, to endure recriminations? What if we who claim the Christian martyrs refrained from our excuses and left our institutional ghettos as did Martin Luther King, Jr., Alan Boesak, Etty Hillesum, Fannie Lou Homer, crossing boundaries and joining other pilgrims who have had a vision of a new humanity?

When we break the Eucharistic bread, we pronounce our opposition to the forces of evil, to violence, to poverty. "It takes far more courage to walk into a violent situation voluntarily, knowing that suffering is virtually inevitable, choosing to draw the poison of the violence with one's own body rather than perpetuating the downward spiral of hate. But that way of the cross, Jesus' way, is what we celebrate in every Eucharist."[14] The Eucharist makes us one with those whose deaths shock us and whose suffering haunts us. In order not to belie its meaning, we must make our resources, our reputations, our lives, part of our pledge. The Eucharist challenges us to dispute the present order of things and to create an alternative future. "I despise your feasts and I take no delight in your solemn assemblies. . . . Rather, let justice roll down like waters" (Amos 5:21-4).

We are people of the Incarnation, crucifixion, and resurrection. In the here and now of God's realm we are overwhelmed by the scale and scope of human suffering. But in faith we know that suffering produces hope. Goliath-structures produce Davids. Anguished parents among us authorize the use of organs from their dead child, so that another child may live. Small communities of young people pierce the darkness around us with the light of their prayer and their protest. The slow stream of medical workers continues to flow into remote camps and outposts, and healing happens. Terminal AIDS sufferers and their friends and families teach us how to face death.

Tiny seeds yield abundant fruit. There is a power in weakness that we who are Christians are supposed to understand. Jesus said it in many ways. If you love your life, you will lose it. If you say you can see, you are blind. The littlest among you is the greatest. The secret of Christian hope is the freedom to be truly alive even in the face of death. "What seems to have made Jesus of Nazareth so distinctive in the eyes of his fellow Galileans was his intense aliveness."[15] Amid the tortures of his own crucifixion, he was still offering hope to a fellow sufferer.

That is why the struggles of Christians in today's world are so powerful. The mass resettlement policies of South Africa are bringing the church into the front lines of the politics of apartheid. The base communities of Latin America are bringing the church into slums and shanty towns, but more importantly, are bringing the church to conversion. The church is being purified and reborn. Today's martyrs speak eloquently about the power of a community to face diminishment, even death.

In our hearts we know that the blame for human suffering

lies not on God's shoulders, but on ours, for the misuse and abuse of life and its resources. In our better moments we enter the pool of compassion and take our shift in the struggle. The church emerging today is not a church set apart for worship, not a church keen on making judgments, but a church at the center, carrying human grief and pain, bearing scorn and rejection.

We stand on our belief in the resurrection, even as evils threaten to erode it: the downing of an Iranian passenger plane, senseless political murders, the slow deaths of our forests and lakes. We take courage from our companions, whether they march in distant cities, pray in other languages, extend their aching arms across unknown cultures and creeds.

Our heartache is world-size, but it reverberates in the most private parts of our psyches. Each birth in poverty and each refugee family is more than a story. Each rigged trial and cruel torture is more than a story. Each death of each innocent victim, the pawn of politics and greed and power, is more than a story. How important it is that individually and corporately we protect, defend, and choose life: so that the resurrection is more than a story!

✳ 7 ✳

Prophets in Our Own House

I stood at the fence, one night in September, feet rooted
to the muddy ground, hands deep in my pockets,
watching through the wire that flat, ravaged land . . .
imagining through the fence a field of bracken and
scrub, a field of flowers, a field of corn, a field of children playing . . . A hundred yards to my left, women
cut the wire. . . . Women waiting, watching, just being
there, behaving as if peace were possible, living our
dream of the future now.[1]

At Greenham Common, the impossible became the possible.
The missiles will be removed, the base will close, and something creative can once again grow on that "flat, ravaged
land." Most of the prophets we know by name are men. There
is the Old Testament hall of fame: Isaiah, Daniel, the unique

voice of John the Baptist, the long line of radicals from Augustine to Francis of Assisi, Martin Luther and John Wesley, Francis Xavier and Thomas More, all the way to Mohandas Gandhi, Daniel Berrigan, Oscar Romero, and Steve Biko. Of course, there have always been women who challenged the status quo and who spoke and lived the truth of their convictions. We are beginning now to name them: Deborah, Hannah, Lydia, Catherine of Siena, Sojourner Truth, Simone Weil, Karen Silkwood. It is significant, however, that the author of the quotation above is not named. She is one of the Greenham Common women. Like the mothers of Argentina, the women of northern Ireland, the religious sisterhoods of the United States, the women strikers of Malaysia. The Greenham Common community is a symbol of the prophetic presence of women in our contemporary society.

Perhaps because the Christian churches have been so dominantly male in their leadership, women are casting the light of their faith in arenas that stretch across boundaries of church and society. Some years ago certain prophets proclaimed the death of God, the death of the God of narrow doctrine, of an exclusively Western bias, the God of private religion and individualistic piety. In a very real way, prophets today, and indeed women prophets, are proclaiming the death of the church, a church that is exclusive, hierarchically and patriarchically constituted, a church that is a "federation of denominations."[2] Today's prophets are announcing a church that is open to the wider oikoumene, a church that is inclusive, incarnational, global, interconnected. Often it is women who are the witnesses to this new reality, to this emerging church. "We must engage in a struggle for the church of the poor, the church of the Third World, the church of women. Unless all these elements of church come into full bloom and become conscious, we will not have the catholic church."[3] A prophet is a witness in a twofold sense, taking in the concrete situation (as an interested spectator witnesses a street scene), and behaving as if another reality were possible (as an interracial marriage witnesses to the unity of the human family). The prophet is a person involved in timely turmoil and vested in its future. But a person with a vision of how it could be, how a daring transformation might occur.

The Christian prophet is a radical in a twofold sense as well, rooted in the here and now, in a particular history and tradition, but also rooted in a Biblical perspective, which envisions the unfolding of the reign of God. Christian prophets know their true situation, "I am the vine, you are the branches . . . apart from me you can do nothing" (John 15:5). They have been grasped by God. Events and circumstances have led them to a turning point that required a surrender, a letting go. They are no longer really in charge of the mission at hand. Their responses and their words come from a source deep within. And they are impelled to turn often toward that source, for energy and strength. They give themselves over to the project of God. How else could we account for Dorothy Day's personal risks, for the endurance of Winnie and Nelson Mandela, and for the hardships undertaken by those who have resisted military and political tyranny? "The only thing that prophets have in common is that they have been sent, and the mission on which they are sent is not theirs, nor is the power theirs that gives them strength and patience and courage and makes them indifferent to the opinions of other people."[4]

Mary of Nazareth was an unlikely candidate for prophecy. Yet it was she who announced God's faithful ushering in of a new order of things. "God's mercy is from age to age, on those who show respect." And it was she who warned the proud, the mighty, the rich, of the precariousness of their thrones and their coffers. It is unfortunate that the only Mary many Christians have met is the trivialized and insipid Mary of our statues.

Prophets are those who open new paths, who dream aloud, and who dare to be different. They may be eloquent; they may be eccentric. "Prophecy," writes J. V. Taylor, "is essentially an act of recognition by which one sees the significance of an event as a revelation which must be passed on."[5] The founders of religious orders, men and women, were such visionaries.

The challenge to their twentieth-century followers is to rediscover those charisms and embody them afresh. Sometimes it is easier to launch a new movement than to revitalize one that has become lethargic and atrophied. Are the new religious orders of our day: the Quakers, the Catholic Workers, the movement for the ordination of women, the Sanctuary workers, the anti-apartheid organizations? Similarly, the Protestant reformers had a message to convey. The challenge today is to recognize the insularity of club churches and to honor the centrality and ecumenicity of mission.

The Greek word for "prophet" means "one who speaks." But certainly not in a dull drone or in an unimaginative oratory. The character of prophecy includes urgency and action, determination, poetry, and enthusiasm. I remember walking into a lecture hall where a young prophet was stirring college students with his radical cries for draft resistance. I felt the same electricity in the room where Liz McAllister was warning against the imminent dangers of nuclear testing. And prophecy is not by word alone. Ribbons and photos and poems have dangled from the wire fences at Greenham Common. Blacks used their bodies in lunchrooms and on buses during the United States civil rights efforts of the 1960s. Women in India have stopped bulldozers by embracing the threatened trees. Jail cells have long been the pulpits and the platforms of prophets.

The message of the prophet arises out of the concrete affairs of human life, idolatry, oppression, neglect, waste—and returns to specific situations in the form of alternative behavior, movements of liberation and repentance, and creative solutions. Leviticus spoke of a year of jubilee. Isaiah described a new kind of fast and a new form of worship. Jeremiah learned from the potter. John the Baptist cried out from the desert. Mary stood steadfast at the foot of the cross. There is no one way to prophesy. But whatever form the message takes, it will shock those who resist it and ensure disapproval and controversy for the messenger.

When Jesus stood up in the synagogue in Nazareth and told his hearers that Isaiah's prophecy was his as well, they marveled. At first they marveled at his cleverness and his gusto. But when they realized that he was serious about rescuing captives and restoring sight to the blind, that his words had implications, they were irate. They wanted to expel him. Prophets are not popular for long. I have one clear memory of a situation in which I dared to speak a difficult truth publicly and found myself expelled. Suddenly I was alone. Even those who agreed with me kept silent. In Milwaukee we speak of Bishop Rembert Weakland's courage, and also of his lost chances for political promotion. Theresa Kane faced her own expulsion after she confronted John Paul II with her prophetic message. And my frame of reference includes the Hunthausens, the Currans, the Mansours, the IHMs, and indeed many Roman Catholic women of the United States.

Something is terribly distorted in the life of our churches when the prophets are being expelled. Unless of course we are ready to disavow the integrity and the viability of our church structures and church authority. Jesus spoke his reminder of harrassment to his followers, "They will harry you as they harried me. They will respect your words as much as they respected mine" (John 15:20). Some credibility will always be lacking in the prophetic voice of our churches until our own prophets are respected and heard. Yes, they may be tested; and some of them may be false. But crucial to all our efforts to proclaim God's reign is our acceptance of those who grow up among us as thorns and gadflies. The stone rejected may well be the cornerstone.

It has always been the vocation of the church to accompany the poor and to defend those who are unjustly treated. No one who claims to be Christian argues with this prophetic stance. There are differences though in our approach to living out this vocation. Church history is blotched with the shame of its own abuses, of power and of resources. It is far easier to decry injustice than to actively resist it. We are better at statements supporting those who suffer than at suffering ourselves on their behalf. At the same time, we are learning from the poor and oppressed. At least in some places, prophets are arising from within the Christian community and from within society at large. "In practice we have invented a god that sanctifies the system....It is the same capricious, blind, and mute idol that produces the scandalous wealth of a fat developed world at the expense of the exploitation, robbery and death of people in Chile, Haiti, Paraguay....That god wraps himself with any flag . . . or disguises himself with religious piety."[6] These are the words of a woman in exile, banished by forces that reject the political implications of her religious beliefs. Another female prophet wrote in 1984:

> The church is not the leading force in the movement of resistance in the Philippines. . . . It is not the church as a whole or as an institution that is doing the prophetic action but church people and church groups, sometimes even in conflict with church authorities and institutions....There is need of working towards the vision of a really new society and a new church. [7]

And a third woman testifies, "I think there is a growth of faith in new forms all over the world, and some of the signs of it are very classical signs, base communities, martyrdom. . . . The price to be a Christian will be higher in the next twenty years."[8]

These are the voices of ecumenical women. Members of Greenpeace, the United Farmworkers, and Oxfam are not greatly concerned with doctrinal differences and ecclesiastical sanctions. Solidarity with those in need is basic to the faith and the common commitment of anonymous Christians everywhere. Their primary agenda is the humanizing of situations that diminish and destroy life.

Professional training in Germany deepened the awareness of the challenges that Indian sisters in my community face. After more than ten years of rich opportunities and relative comfort in Europe, they subsequently found the demands of village work and the exigencies of nursing in India harsh realities. Medicines are scarce, travel is rough and time consuming. Desperate poverty and relentless need haunt every day of their ministry. That few of those who surround them are Christian is of no consequence. The sisters weave a patient pattern of assistance, friendship, and respect for religious tradition. They do not have the luxury of club security.

Implicit in today's prophetic witness is the call to self-criticism and to a constant renewal of sacrosanct structures and carefully guarded lifestyles. One ground of hope for the church is its slow realization that we must "carry about in our bodies the dying of Jesus, so that in our bodies the life of Jesus may also be revealed" (2 Corinthians 4:10). The missionary character of the new church requires a stripping of our protective cloisters, our discriminating structures, our self-justified security, and all those agendas that divide and weaken our attention. How else will we be free enough to recognize the God of the poor, and unencumbered enough to be companion to the disinherited? Our words are hollow and our efforts for unity are futile until we apply to ourselves the eloquent and adamant sermons that we preach. "They seek me day after day, and desire to know my ways....Remove from your midst oppression... bestow your bread on the hungry and satisfy the afflicted...then your wound will quickly be healed...then you shall call and the Lord will answer" (Isaiah 58:2, 8-10).

The basic ingredients of politics are power and participation. However much the church denies its meddling in politics, the issues of power and participation cannot be ignored. No wonder that women are the spokespersons of a renewed and liberating church. In many instances it is they who have been denied access to either power or participation. At the same time it is they who have been silent nurturers of the faith, anxious for the spiritual lives of their children, passing on the legacy of the Scriptures, forming the worshipping communities in places as dissimilar as Moscow, Bristol, and Bombay. Within the church itself, it may be women who can correct the balance between the exercise of power and the ministry of service, between the truth of tradition and the fruitful exchange that participation enables. Is that not the underlying meaning of some of the reversals and symbolic actions we are seeing, women breaking bread and sharing the cup, women revising the language of a male church, women supporting their daughters' pursuit of ordination, women gathering in support of the mothers of the West Bank, the prostitutes of Manila, the garment workers of Texas? It may, perhaps must, begin with anger. One woman describes her own evolution, "I am angry at women in church and society being silenced, at the way they are constantly being robbed of their own spiritual and emotional viewpoint."[9] If anger is the starting point, courage is the long journey into change.

There seems to be an easy transition for women, awakened to their own strengths and dignity, to arenas of justice and freedom for the whole of society. "Everything begins in mysticism," says the poet, "and ends in politics." Our churches have been relatively successful in separating spirituality from politics. Women often take the lead in bridging the gap. Spirituality integrates our sacred and secular history. Our Christian vocation is not merely one of the "varieties of religious experience." It is the whetstone against which we question every event and every issue of our day. Engagement, rather than withdrawal, is the responsibility of the Christian community. God has claimed the whole of the inhabited earth, and it is within and among its evils, its crises, its cultures, and its opportunities for exchange, that we live out our Christian calling.

The challenge to all of us, and to women in particular, as we achieve greater accessibility to positions of authority in the church and in society, is to cast a new perspective on old issues. For too long we have worshipped more than one god. For too long we have been idolatrously preoccupied with war, material wealth, with a number-one position (from the America's Cup in yachting to supremacy in space). It is right and good that we ask sharp questions about the meaning of security. Are the Communists, in the Soviet Union or in Cuba, our greatest enemies? Or are we making enemies of those closer to us, the desperate jobless turned criminal, the frightened property owner turned vigilante, the disillusioned youth turned gang member? Can security be the fruit of greater and more subtle violence? It is right and good that we bring into closer scrutiny, realities that are inseparably related, the grain surplus of the West and famine in other parts of the world, the budget figures for defense and those for health care and job training, government restrictions on the media and runaway foreign policy. Can we afford to build larger barns to store our surplus when the very gift of life is at stake? Why are many of us morally indignant at "sins of the flesh" and morally inert over the carnage of warfare? Can competition ever have lasting beneficial effects if it is not balanced with, and sometimes abandoned for, cooperation?

Each segment of the Scriptures is cast amid historical events and earthly realities. The checkered history of the Israelites is the backdrop for their worship and their obedience, their waywardness and sin. The psalms are the cries of actual people facing actual crises. The books of the prophets are as much an account of current events as they are of personal vocations. Jesus taught and healed within the limits of geography and culture and history. Paul's letter to Corinth details the issues that faced those recent converts. Religion and spirituality are mere escapes if they do not provide the underlying framework and perspective from which every current event and issue is viewed and judged. Membership in the church is only a refuge if it does not commit us to shape political and social structures and to support the building of a just and peaceful society. The Christian cannot be indifferent to any of the forces that mold and influence human life. How to respond to current events, and with what degree of prayer and discipline, are relevant subjects for our church communities. Becoming missionaries within our own local setting, proclaiming in speech and in action that all authority comes from God and all of creation is designed to be obedient to God's purposes—this is the prophetic role of the church.

The Scriptures can be lifted from the tombs of their trite interpretation. Fresh meaning can be given to familiar feasts and well-worn verses. Nebuchadnezzar's furnace and Herod's vengeful sword are no less threatening to today's innocents. Each Christian community, in the spirit of Hebrews, can compile its own stories of faith. We can dramatize with our own heroines the accounts of Shiprah and Puah, Joanna, Tabitha, and the early Christian house churches.

Both our spirituality and our politics require constant uprooting and re-radicalizing toward deeper sensitivity and compassion. It may be that women's experiences lead in this direction more naturally and spontaneously than men's.

In the gospel of Mark, a succinct description of Jesus tells a long story. "They found him too much for them." This person was one whom they had to beg to leave them because he was so honest and so radical. Whom they mistrusted because he seemed to know them better than they knew themselves. Whom they snubbed because he was so ordinary and so human. Monica Furlong suggests that the kind of prophecy needed today is calling people "to be simply human at a time when this is anything but easy for most people."[10] Not unlike Jesus' neighbors and relatives, religious-minded men and women today are shocked by honesty and unimpressed by simplicity.

We have moved the center of attention from the Christian community and the laity to certain distinct personalities and officials. We have lost the common touch, the significance of community meals, the beauty of family blessings, the profound lessons of creation with its cycles and patterns. Mimicking society's standards, we have honored too exclusively those who have been ambitious, articulate, or academic. We have begun to look skeptically at the energy and bustle of a large family, at the simple but satisfying life of rural people, at the dreams of youth for a more communal lifestyle in harmony with nature. Our parish units and autonomous congregations do not foster a sense of belonging to a universal church, do not encourage an ecumenical exchange of culture and charism. We live side by side and work side by side with a variety of ethnic and social backgrounds; but for our spiritual support and nourishment, we rely on a homogeneous assembly.

We completely lose sight that prophets and peacemakers,

community-builders and leaders, the simply human and the simply just, live outside our church boundaries as well as within. In fact, many of them have tested the institution and found it hypocritical and irrelevant. We have succumbed, perhaps excessively, to the management techniques and the goal and planning processes of business and industry. Our ministries, too, are shaped and directed by commissions and five-year projections. Actual human need is not always the impetus or the criterion.

Perhaps a revelation for today is the slow emergence of lay leadership, lay participation, and lay spirituality that parallels and is sometimes integrated with the emergence of woman-church and feminist spirituality:

> The church which is life-giving for me is the church which does not rest on the status quo; a church which aligns itself with the poor of our earth; a church which honors people's experiences; a church which is open to dialogue and expression; it is a church which is viewed as a community of believers.[11]

The challenge to this movement is to move deeply enough into the rhythms of action and reflection, prayer and politics, participation and power, so as to avoid some of the mistakes of our institutions: overactivity, superficial and inadequate formation, excessive bureaucracy, and personality cults. The church has new life and significance where it is being returned to the people.

What do these prophetic currents circulating in and around the church say to us about an ecumenical spirituality? They point us toward three qualities of Christian life and renewal: freedom, creativity, and integrity. These are also prophetic qualities.

The church today will be served by people who have achieved an inner freedom. Thomas Merton describes it: "He [or she] has come to experience the ground of his own being in such a way that he knows the secret of liberation and can somehow or other communicate this to others."[12] Such freedom will enable us to discern our obedience within the contexts of our daily lives. And to discern as well the situations in which we are to be disobedient. It will enable us to shed our narrow concepts of membership, to break barriers, to reach out to an inclusive community.

When we choose a larger commitment, we begin to be free of the laws by which we have formerly lived. This free spirit within us will make us flexible and resilient so that our ministry stems from human need and the promptings of the Spirit. We will not be so fettered by considerations of economic advantages, respectability, and public opinion. We will be less likely to betray our own gifts and vocation and more likely to profit by the lesson of the parable of the talents. Such freedom will urge us to speak what we have heard and seen, regardless of criticism or ostracism. "Better for us to obey God than human beings" (Acts 5:29). Perhaps the prophets among us are those who are disobedient.

If the church most of us know is dying, the emerging church will be served by people who are imaginative and creative, those who see and "speak the world differently."[13] Like the prophets before us, we will return to the Scriptures and discover how they are *our* story. We will return to those situations that have stifled us and forced us into exile, and reclaim our heritage, rename our experiences. We will take responsibility in our own cultural and social setting for making the gospel alive and attractive. We will continue to have high expectations of ourselves and of one another, and of what can be renewed and revitalized when we trust and encourage one another. "To the one whose power now at work in us can do immeasurably more than we can ask or imagine—to that one be glory" (Ephesians 3:20-21). Perhaps our prophets are those at the fringes of the institutional church, re-searching, re-claiming and re-constructing.

To be convincing, today's Christians must be convinced. We have grown accustomed to the splits, the rationalizing, and the compromises in our own lives and in our surrounding milieus.

Immersion in the Word of God is necessary to convict us and ensure our integrity. God's Word must become "like fire burning in our hearts, imprisoned in our bones" (Jeremiah 20:9). Jeremiah's crisis will be our own, and either we will abandon our vocation or we will face a radical conversion. Integrity will demand that we accept at last a view of life as mutual interaction and interdependence. When our relationship with the God of all creation is sure enough, our own splits will heal, and our word and deed will be one. When the hallmark of our experience of God is that of a living presence expressing and extending love, then our principal task will be to "keep the power of relationship alive in our world."[14] "We are called to reach out, to deepen relationships, or to right wrong relations—those that deny, distort, or prevent human dignity from arising—as we recall each other into the power of personhood. We are called to journey this way. to stay in and with this radical power of love."[15] "It is love that I desire, not sacrifice, and knowledge of God rather than holocausts" (Hosea 6:6). Perhaps our prophets are those who place the virtue of relationship before prudence and discipline.

And finally, we can join that chorus of voices proclaiming the liberation and restoration of the Zion of our day. "We know, we women, we know all about earnestly desiring and waiting, about loving and suffering and going on anyway, witnesses to a different reality, a different way, an impossible possibility of resurrection."[16]

❋ 8 ❋

Celebrating as a Family

In 1987, my sister-in-law, Kathleen, died after a long confrontation with cancer. Our large clan gathered from all four corners of the United States to mourn and also to celebrate. Funerals have always been occasions for family reunions in my culture and tradition. The youngest member of the clan was Kathleen's own grandson, just a few weeks old. The little ones hovered around the open casket, unexpectedly easy with death, and no doubt relieved to see grandma in colorful dress and surrounded by flowers after their recent grim visits to a hospital bed. Of course we told stories as we waited with one another for that final farewell. And we reminisced as we met relatives and caught up with childhood friends. Kathleen's five daughters were selecting significant readings and hymns for the funeral Mass. My brother was conferring with the priest about the sermon's contents. There were two days of praying, laughing, crying, caring for one another. We gathered up the highlights of Kathleen's life, pointed ourselves toward the future, and held the present moment lovingly and reverently. Solemn and sad as the occasion was, it was also a time for celebrating, giving thanks, and remembering.

Are these not the ingredients of all family reunions, the paradigms of our gatherings in faith as congregations, as praying communities, as the people of God, and more so, the family of God? Only human beings celebrate, Harvey Cox said in his famous *Feast of Fools*. Celebrating is part of the natural rhythm of our lives, honoring past experiences, looking forward to future events, cherishing this special present moment. Our work gives way to weekends, to holidays. Seasons have their peaks: Yuletide, the festival of spring, summer play, harvest time. Our individual lives are a series of passages, marked by celebration, birthdays, commencements, betrothals, anniversaries. And our corporate lives as well: national events, religious feasts, bicentennials, moon landings, and medical breakthroughs. We celebrate our victories and have consolation parties upon our defeats. We celebrate comings and goings, successful surgeries, new job opportunities, the onset of adolescence and of retirement. We seek a balance of effort and relaxation, the humdrum and the comic relief, the workaday world and the Sunday outing. Our personal health and sanity require this balance, and our health and wholeness as a people depend on it as well.

The elements of celebration are universal: guests, music, gifts, refreshments, the shedding of worries and cares. We are freed to be renewed by the humor and affection of close friends, by the new roles into which fun and play cast us. We experience a shift in perspective and a recess from the strains of serious business. For a brief span we are lifted out of ourselves, out of time, into a timeless transcendence, into mystery and fantasy. Not the least effect is the deepening of our human bonds, woven tightly through common emotion, excitement, and ecstasy.

"To play," says Hugo Rahner, "is to yield oneself to a kind of magic, to give the lie to the inconvenient world of fact . . . the mind is prepared to accept the unimagined and incredible, to enter a world where different laws apply, to be relieved of all the weights that bear it down, to be free...."[1] There are profound connections between prayer and play. Prayer, too, bridges the past and the future, takes us into the unimagined and the incredible, lifts us out of ourselves into a transcendent world of mystery and hope. Our faith is the entrance into a secret energy that restores the human spirit, shifts our perspective, and reminds us of the total drama of the current scene. Worship is the celebration of the totality of life.

Bonds of love and faith are the foundation for prayer and worship. Because of those bonds, both young and old, traditional and ultra-modern, even those distantly apart, can meet and unite. It is family prayer, whether it be a house church, a base community, a congregation, an ecumenical gathering. In reality or by intent, all those who share a common origin and common destiny are included. Prayer and worship are catholic by their very nature.

Recently, a lay church minister related a story all too familiar in our Christian experience. Her local church was undergoing a period of growth and renewal after the visit of a charismatic Franciscan. Elements were creeping back into the church that had been lost or alienated: young people, livelier liturgies, testimonies of healing and conversion, family agendas. Those who had worshipped there and had claims on the style and manner of traditional worship were perturbed and resistant. A struggle ensued, the vicar could not bridge the tension, and the new momentum was broken. Before long, the church returned to its previous dull and diminished existence. The plea of this lay woman was earnest and agonized: Our church family must accommodate and embrace *all* its children!

When we come together to pray and to worship, we are all on an equal footing. Especially in that context, our differences exist only for the purpose of exchange. Ministerial roles serve the assembly by facilitating and binding together our movements of intercession, communion, and thanksgiving. In the presence of God, we are stripped of our hierarchical trappings, our denominational titles, our erudition, and our unworthiness. We are family, uniting to remember, to celebrate, and to give thanks. We depart more conscious of our unity, more prepared for the ongoing trials, more willing to be priest and prophet and place of exchange in our daily lives.

Questions, however, haunt us. Does our ecumenical prayer make us more one? Is there more human community among us as a result? Are we more than strangers huddled in an upper room? After years of common ecumenical prayer, are we any different, any closer to mutual understanding and acceptance? Has an exchange of charisms influenced our own denominational pattern of prayer and worship? Do we merely pretend to pray together and immediately revert to our own prayer menus? Do we believe that we have truly worshipped when we participate in another tradition's Eucharist? Are we more conscientious than God in sorting out paraliturgy, Holy Communion service, and authentic Eucharist?

Just as prayer and play have much in common, so should our holy meals reveal their links with their social counterparts. Our churches are our larger homes, the place where we celebrate our faith heritage and faith ties. It was an ordinary meal that Jesus shared with Mary and Martha in Bethany, with Simon the Pharisee, with the disciples at Emmaus, and later on the beach. But there is no doubt that those meals were extensions of the Last Supper as examples of the full meaning of the gift of exchange. It takes many meals to re-enact the multiple levels of service and self-gift. It takes the celebrations of sari-clad worshippers in South India, of small congregations in ancient churches in rural Norfolk, of lively inner-city parishes, of student campus groups. It takes the solemn three-hour Eucharist in an Orthodox cathedral and the solemn hasty communion of catechists in a Central American barrio. It takes the bread broken and passed on the steps of the federal building after a nuclear protest march, the food served in the downtown meal hall, the evening community casserole, the Christmas dinner eaten with friends and family. Each one makes a statement about our faith. Each one entails a commitment to care for one another. Our holy meals converge around creation, human commitments, our faith witness. They become one sign in the bread we break and the cup we drink.

Our worship must be created and conducted so that each part of the community can find itself in it, identify with its language, or symbolism or style, participate in its unfolding, and benefit from its blessings. The drama we enact must be "large enough" that everyone can play a part, grasp something of the meaning, enter into the exchange. It must include our past saints and heroes, our current questions and crises, a vision of the world we want to fashion. It must enlarge the walls of our churches so that our community reaches from one end of the earth to the other. Nothing that concerns the human family is foreign to our prayer. The God we address must be named in every tongue and described in every image available to human minds. We must not put limits on the breadth and height and depth of God's embrace, or on the potential of the community to be a local incarnation of the universal church.

Mark Gibbs has voiced the concern of many Christians who find that church services are unappealing because they are irrelevant to their daily lives and dilemmas.[2] He speaks of men and women engaged in secular occupations, competitive careers, political activities. Many have deserted the mainline churches except for a rare attendance at a funeral or a major church festival. Many are trying to discover their own styles of praying and discerning Christian values within their Monday to Friday responsibilities. They no longer expect that their spiritual journeys will be incorporated or affirmed in regular church worship. For them and for many of our youth, mesmerized by the variety and excitement of modern media, church rituals are meaningless and embarrassing. Countless Christians are caught in the chasm between traditional practices to which they sentimentally adhere and a vacuum of relevant spiritual direction.

We need ritual as a social expression. We all respond to the spine-tingling moments when the Olympic medals are distributed. Or to the solemnity of a state funeral or a presidential inauguration. Even in our families we ritualize our christenings, our summer holidays, our methods of communicating. But "enforced ritual, handed down from above, chokes off spontaneity and petrifies the spirit."[3] Is there any wonder that young people reject those ceremonies and customs that represent the faith of another time, but not their own? Thus we have congregations that neither sing nor respond orally to the prayers. Sacraments are either neglected or entered into out of a sense of obligation. Family meal prayers are uncommon, and where they persist, they are often trite or mere formulas. Some people are straddling dead rituals and the implications of surrendering them. Young couples choose a church wedding simply because the setting speaks more eloquently and provides more pageantry. They select baptismal sponsors for their babies, whether or not the same actually participate in the life of the church.

We are challenged to create and accept new rituals that will nourish contemporary faith and give access to a wide range of religious experience. And not only rituals, but experiences of prayer, retreat, discernment, and celebration. It is necessary to break out of our church contexts and step into the actual environments where faith is tested and practiced. To relocate ceremonies and services where they touch the complex lives of today's Christians. The way of the cross enacted in our city streets may do more to "convict" us than a procession inside our churches. A sunrise service at a lakeside or in an open field may resurrect our fervor more deeply than a solemn cathedral service. We are more in need of training in the skills of conversion than we are of further information or instruction. It is time to rethink our Lenten ascetical practices and our marriage catechesis. In my own tradition, we have largely let go of patronal feasts, rogation days, litanies, and novenas. But we have not replaced them with sufficient expressions of faith to nourish and inspire today's believers.

Rituals must be renewed so that they express the longings

and the struggles of students, the divorced, the single, those in ecumenical marriages. We need more animators of liturgy, fewer controlling functionaries. The world must be more present in our sanctuaries, its concerns more evident in our penitential rites. We need to distinguish between basic liturgical rites and language, and ceremonies and prayers that can be adapted to specific occasions and uses. "In the old way of doing things, the objects of blessings were bread, good weather for the harvest, healthy cattle, the averting of a plague, protection against a storm."[4] Today we search for blessings and rituals that will keep family members united, protect us from nuclear accident, safeguard our rivers and streams, guide our experiments in genetic engineering and disease control. Even our postures at prayer need rethinking. We are more conscious today of the impact of body language, as we are of inclusive language and intercultural sensitivities.

Recently a friend and I spent time in the home of two elderly women. One has a hearing impairment. Both are deeply Christian. They took us by surprise when they suggested that we sit together in front of the fire in silence as our communal prayer. We sat in each other's presence for thirty minutes, drinking deeply of the richness of our combined solitudes. It was a ritual that was ideal for those circumstances.

Our images of God are expanding. The Latin American church has helped us: the peasant Christ with calloused hands and sweaty brow, Christ the worker, the God of the poor, hunted, and tortured. Women are contributing new faces of God and new attributes: tenderness, fidelity, the weaver-woman image, the baker-God. In our day God is imprisoned, on trial, in exile, keeping vigil, serving soup, blessing our peace camps.

Implicit in all this is a rediscovery of the connections between ordinary Christian life and our liturgical seasons, sacraments, and observances. In many churches the gap is wide between the age-old practices of a tradition and the constantly changing circumstances of contemporary life, between developments in theology and spirituality and the inadequate formation offered lay Christians, between the assumptions of church ministers and the actual yearnings of lay men and women. How do we affirm the faith of harrassed families, of confident, competent women, of media-fed youth, of frustrated traditional church members? Affirm it and encourage its multiple expressions?

Jesus was a marvelous teacher, adept at taking the simple events of life and weaving them into parables and images of the spiritual life, planting and reaping, building a house, offering hospitality, hiring workers. Teaching is making connections. Within the most commonplace experience, Jesus was able to point to the truth of our Christian vocation: Who is your neighbor? Who are my mother and my brothers? Little children, whitewashed tombs, deserts, and mercenary shepherds made spiritual direction concrete and clear. What are the images that will address the hopes and joys, griefs and anxieties of men and women today? How do we weave into our liturgies famines and fasting, care for the environment and blatant waste, violence, leisure, and the many concerns of those who come to worship? Would not Jesus' Sermon on the Mount, if preached today, present a world we recognized? Could we in the West not find parables for our sermons in budget making, gardening, camping, and the vast array of experiences familiar to our congregations? With encouragement, persons in our assemblies could share their own faith journeys, actual discernments, and decisions. The Quaker view of ministry challenges us: Let the one who is on fire ignite others. We do an injustice both to our ordained ministers and to the people of God by our narrow expectations of preaching.

I am reminded of a sermon I heard recently. The text was that of Noah and the great flood, culminating in God's covenant with humanity. God would never again allow the waters to destroy the earth. That morning's news had described the floods that inundated parts of Rio de Janeiro, killing many and making thousands homeless. What could the sermon possibly mean to those who had heard the news? Yet no reference, no connection, was made. We wonder why faith and life are separated, why people see so little relevance of religion in their daily lives.

For many of us the liturgical year, with its seasons and feasts, is rich in the way it leads us to a constant renewal of life and commitment. Often, however, that movement becomes sterile and monotonous. Year after year we take on lenten penances, stand listlessly through the reading of the Passion, hear the amazing accounts of Pentecost, minimally observe the Week of Prayer for Christian Unity. We lack the insights and the skills to interpret and integrate our faith with our lifestyles, choices, priorities. We do not enter the stream deeply enough to be renewed and transformed.

Happily there is a growing consciousness of the need for a more spontaneous and flexible expression of faith and practice. From the Sojourners community in the United States to Christians in Sri Lanka, new approaches in spirituality are integrating prayer and action. We are learning to incorporate the music, symbols, and dance of various cultures into our worship. Poets like Chuck Lathrop, Denise Levertov, Cecil Rajendra, and Julia Esquivel are bringing the gospel into new arenas and translating it for today's radicals.

But most of these translations do not reach average churchgoers who are still dependent on a pastor or bishop to bring information and issues to their attention. One need only look at the pamphlet racks in many of our churches or read the notice boards. There is an appalling dearth of challenging material and a distorted emphasis on internal church affairs, from flower rotas to spaghetti dinners.

We who are serious about an ecumenical spirituality rooted in and nourished by prayer and worship must re-examine the basic ingredients of celebration: a spirit of reflection and rememberance, spontaneous praise and rejoicing, humble gratitude for every good gift.

The ability to contemplate, to appreciate the goodness and beauty of life and of creation, is at the heart of our celebration. Contemplation begins with wonder and leads to wisdom. We come to perceive connections and larger patterns in reality, to probe the hungers and yearnings of human hearts, and to respond to life with awareness and sensitivity.

We have narrowed, however, the meaning of contemplation and made it a specialty of a few professionals. We view it as an indulgence practiced by graduates of prayer and meditation, rather than the most elementary expression of our religious experience. Contemplation is closely linked with nature, with the simple things of life, with breath itself. Earth is an altar on which we offer the work of our hands and minds. Bread symbolizes our hungers, and wine our pains and joys. Spring and rebirth are theological events; every part of nature is a source of revelation. "Just to be is a blessing," said Abraham Heschel, "just to live is holy." A wise father has said that every parent of a newborn has entered the school of contemplation. We find the contemplative spirit flourishing in the hearts of woodcutters and artists, of naturalists and those who cope with declining health. Their experiences yield secrets hidden from those who live complicated and frenzied lives. We may not all have the poetic facility of an e.e. cummings or a Gerard Manley Hopkins, but we respond with awe and wonder to the first streaks of dawn, the dew on fragile flowers, the swift freedom on skis on snow, the pure sounds of a flute. How can we restore or enhance this gift of contemplation as an integral part of our spiritual renewal? What is the place of silence and quiet meditation in our traditions, our church services, our community life? We in the West are verbose. We read, recite, sermonize, sing hymns, make intercessions, pray psalms, and use speech even compulsively. There is little affirmation in our communal worship of silence and space.

We have within our grasp the materials for reflection. Our liturgies are rife with mantras, a meditative prayer form well known in the East: Holy, holy, holy; *Kyrie eleison*; Yours is the kingdom and the power and the glory. We have antiphons and litanies to deepen our sense of the sacred and of an abiding presence. We could restore the psalms as spontaneous, heartfelt prayers of joy, sorrow, fear, and despair.

When we gather in our local settings as the family of God,

we can remember those who are absent, those who have nourished our faith, those who rely upon our prayers and presence. We might include in our opening rites a time of silence and of gathering so that our circles widen around an "invisible cloud of witnesses." We can bring together in our architecture and our physical arrangements the simplicity of natural beauty and the solemnity of religious art. We can maximize and share our retreat centers, our convents, our private chapels. Intensely occupied urban Christians hunger for a time and a space to be alone and for the understanding of the adjustment that requires.

In the United Kingdom, a popular religious television program is a Sunday evening "Songs of Praise." Whether it is nostalgia or search, people are finding inspiration in stories and songs of faith. In our Christian circles, we find ourselves looking to Negro spirituals, to protest poetry and music, to Celtic blessings, Indian *bhajans*, and to the Ecumenical Prayer Cycle for ways to sing and celebrate our interrelatedness.

We Westerners have much to learn from other cultures about the significance of color and dress, dance and musical instruments. Our churches are still relatively conventional and controlled, even in our most festive seasons. In our emphasis on the intellectual, we neglect the sensual and emotional. A dearth of imagination and festivity has contributed to the dying of our churches. Part of the reason for the development and growth of the independent churches of Africa, of the charismatics and the pentecostals, is that many are starved for elements such as indigenous music, drama and dance, expressive rites and customs. The routine liturgies of the mainline churches of the West often reduce the life and energy of congregations. Our alleluias are weak and short-lived. We do not experience the liturgy as a movement in which we are caught up, which traces the patterns of our shared lives, which renews our instincts for community and celebration. Is this not a reason as well for the exaggerated appeal of television evangelists and multimedia religious events?

In some cultures it is precisely in the midst of pain and tragedy that a spirit of celebration and rejoicing erupts. Funerals in South Africa, with their singing and dancing, deepen a sense of solidarity. Dance plays an important part in the healing rituals of Amerindians. In the face of the catastrophes confronting today's world, our churches are challenged to celebrate in vivid and evocative ways the mysterious movement from death to life. What are the songs and prayers that will see us through these uncertain times?

And where today in our Western societies are we most likely to hear rejoicing strains? Perhaps in the deserts of Nevada at the nuclear testing grounds where today's Isaiahs make their prophetic witness. At the doors of the Ministry of Defense where today's high priests enact their rituals of exorcism. In gatherings of women where new tales are told of exodus and liberation. In homes and meeting places where the essential liturgy of the Eucharist is one with the actual struggles of today's disciples. A joyful song rises from the lips of God's multicultured family when the *oikoumene* gather. But not as likely from our subdued and lackluster Sunday morning congregations.

Throughout our pilgrimage, around the year, God is with us, Emmanuel. It is reason enough to rejoice. Praise rings out today from oppressed African townships, destitute Peruvian villages, distant Sri Lankan temples, the open fields of Taizé. If we believe that God's dwelling is among us and that God makes all things new, what can prevent us from joining the chorus?

When Amerindians pray, they turn to the four directions of Mother Earth. When they greet one another, they bow to the innermost depths of the other's being, where truth and love reside. Humble gratitude is the proper attitude of the praying Christian. All is gift. All is grace. We come with open hands to the blessings of creation, to the vast array of human qualities that have enriched our history, to the deep mysteries of our faith. And the God of all gives all to us.

In our worship services in the West we customarily offer money as a sign of gratitude. Its symbolism is long documented. But the needs we gather in prayer are so many and so diverse. Could not our gifts be equally imaginative and varied? As fruit and rice, flowers and incense are expressions of thanksgiving in the East, what are the additional symbols that represent us?

I will always remember my first arrival at one of our convents in India. As the jeep neared the gate of the compound, the horn sounded, and faces appeared from doorways and garden plots. I found myself in a human circle with garlands of fresh flowers around my neck. There was laughter and warmth, a bevy of excitement and incomprehensible exclamations. Before I could respond, I was whisked off to the little chapel, where we stood barefoot and sang a *Te Deum* of thanksgiving. Though I had never before set eyes on those sisters, I had been taken home to them safely, and God was first of all to be thanked.

Thanksgiving Day in the United States is a family day. Wherever possible, the clan gathers, from oldest to youngest, and the most elaborate meal of the year is served. It is hoped that on that day no one celebrates alone. The origins of the custom lie in the days when Amerindians offered their intruders gifts of grain and meat. Without these provisions, many more of the early European settlers would have died in a climate that was harsh and formidable. Remembering that era of gracious neighborliness, North Americans still come together as families in a spirit of thanksgiving.

We all cherish homecomings because we are renewed by common memories, by the warmth of one another's presence, by the most recent blessings of Providence, and by our combined visions of a better future. When will the church become that welcoming, gathering place in which all of God's family will find themselves at home? When will every gift offered, however simple, however unique, be taken up, blessed, and shared? When will our Eucharists more faithfully resemble a family celebration, around a family table, providing a foretaste of the feast we all await? When will our celebrations be so Catholic that we become, in our small assemblies, a representative family of God, a public *Te Deum*?

Notes

Introduction

1. *The Shape of the Church To Come*, trans. Edward Quinn, London: SPCK, 1974, 24.

2. Simon Barrington-Ward, "A New Belonging," CMS Newsletter, July, 1979.

Chapter 1: Hearts Set on the Pilgrimage

1. *Lumen Gentium*, 48.

2. From the Talmud.

3. *The Fearful Void*, Philadelphia: Lippincott, 1974.

4. Nov. 17, 1977, sermon.

5. H. A. Williams, *True Resurrection*, New York: Holt, Rinehart and Winston, 1972, 98.

Chapter 2: What Do You Want Me to Do for You?

1. Quoted in *Peacemaking: Day By Day*, Pax Christi, Erie, Pennsylvania: Benet Press, 50.

2. Mary Hunt, *Women—Invisible in Church and Theology*, ed. Elisabeth Schüssler Fiorenza and Mary Collins, Edinburgh: T. and T. Clark, Ltd., 1985, 90.

3. *Everyday Ecumenism*, Geneva: World Council of Churches, 1987, 69.

4. R.S. Thomas, *H'M*, London: Macmillan, 1975, 34.

5. *Feast of Life*, Geneva: World Council of Churches, 1982, 20.

6. John Davies, *Beginning Now*, London: Collins, 1971, 72.

7. Quoted in *Protestant Mystics*, ed. Anne Fremantle, Boston: Little, Brown and Co., 1964, 289.

Chapter 3: Serving and Being Served

1. Expression is from Robert McAfee Brown, *Unexpected News*, Philadelphia: Westminster, 1984.

2. *The Politics of Spirituality*, Philadelphia: Westminster, 1984, 45.

3. *Your Kingdom Come*, Geneva: World Council of Churches, 1980, 166.

4. Ibid., 162.

5. Ibid., 169.

6. Rosemary Haughton, *The Passionate God*, London: Darton, Longman, Todd, 1981, 333–4.

Chapter 4: Speaking the Word Of Life

1. "Wreathed in Flesh and Warm," *Weavings*, Jan./Feb., 1987, 19.

2. Elizabeth Templeton, "The Churches' Mission in a Secularized Europe," Conference of European Churches, Nov. 1987, unpublished paper.

3. R.E.C. Browne, *The Ministry of the Word*, quoted in John Bluck, *Everyday Ecumenism*, 26.

4. John Bluck, *Everyday Ecumenism*, 25.

5. *Hope for Faith*, Geneva: World Council of Churches, 1986, 21–2.

6. Quoted by Ian Fraser, *Reinventing Theology as the People's Work*, London: USPG, 1981, 21.

Chapter 5: Messengers of Reconciliation

1. Swanwick Conference, Aug. 31–Sept. 4, 1987.

2. John Bluck, *Everyday Ecumenism*, 68.

3. *Towards a Quaker View of Sex*, ed. Alistair Heron, London: Friends House, 1963, 36.

4. London: Hodder and Stoughton, 1983, 90.

5. "Some Reflections Towards an Ecumenical Theology of Peace," unpublished paper, 4.

6. Ibid., 6.

7. David Sheppard, *Bias to the Poor*, 71.

Chapter 6: More Than a Story

1. *Jesus Christ —The Life of the World*, A Worship Book, Geneva: World Council of Churches, 1983, 26.

2. W.H. Vanstone, *Love's Endeavour, Love's Expense*, London: Darton, Longman and Todd, 1977, 119–20.

3. Etty Hillesun, *An Interrupted Life*, trans. Arno Pomerans, New York: Pantheon, 1984.

4. "A World Available for Peace," *Sojourners*, Jan., 1988, 25–6.

5. *Waiting on God*, Glasgow: Collins, 1950, 90.

6. *A Spirituality for Our Times*, Report, Geneva: World Council of Churches, 1984, 20.

7. H.A. Williams, *True Resurrection*, London: Michael Beazley Limited, 1972, 145–6.

8. J.V. Taylor, *Weep Not for Me*, Mystic, Conn.: Twenty-Third Publications, 1986, 4.

9. Antoine de Ste. Exupery, *Wind, Sand and Stars*, trans. Lewis Galantiere, Harcourt, Brace and Company, Inc., 1940, 243.

10. Helen Luke, *The Voice Within*, New York: Crossroad, 1984, 93.

11. Quoted by Anne Morrow Lindbergh, *Hour of Gold, Hour of Lead*, New York: Harcourt Brace Jovanovich, 1973, 179.

12. *Your Kingdom Come*, 55.

13. Dorothee Soelle, *Suffering*, trans. Everett R. Kalin, Philadelphia: Fortress Press, 1975.

14. Walter Wink, "My Enemy ... My Destiny," *Sojourners*, Feb. 1987, 35.

15. J.V. Taylor, *Weep Not for Me*, 40.

Chapter 7: Prophets in Our Own House

1. *Bringing the Invisible into the Light*, Quaker Women's Group, London: Quaker Home Services, 1986, 94–5.

2. Lesslie Newbigin, *Foolishness to the Greeks*, Geneva: World Council of Churches, 1986, 146.

3. Elisabeth Schüssler Fiorenza, *The Inside Stories*, ed. Annie Lally Milhaven, Mystic, Conn.: Twenty-Third Publications, 1987, 58.

4. Rosemary Haughton, *The Transformation of Man*, Springfield, Ilinois: Templegate Publishers, 1980, 129.

5. *The Go-Between God*, New York: Oxford University Press,

1972, 69.

6. Julia Esquivel, *Your Kingdom Come,* 54.

7. S. Mary John Mananzan, *International Review of Mission,* Oct., 1984, 406–7.

8. Dorothee Soelle, *Hope for Faith,* 23.

9. Baerbel von Wartenburg-Potter, *We Will Not Hang Up Our Harps,* Geneva: World Council of Churches, 1987, 1.

10. *The End of Our Exploring,* Coward, McCann and Geoghagen, 1973, 185.

11. Patricia Hussey, *The Inside Stories,* 240.

12. *Asian Journal,* New York: New Directions, 1968, 333.

13. Walter Brueggemann, *The Prophetic Imagination,* Philadelphia: Fortress Press, 1983.

14. Beverly Harrison, *Making the Connections,* Boston: Beacon Press, 1985, 21.

15. Ibid., 19.

16. *Bringing the Invisible into the Light,* 96.

Chapter 8: Celebrating as Family

1. *Man at Play,* New York: Herder and Herder, 1967, 65.

2. "Spiritual Maturity Is for the Laity Too," *Ecumenical Review,* Jan. 1986, 61.

3. Harvey Cox, *Feast of Fools,* New York: Harper & Row, 1969, 71.

4. Fulbert Steffensky, "The Catholicism of the Common People," *Ecumenical Review,* Jan. 1986, 15.

Critical Acclaim for...*A Spirituality of Compassion* by Joan Puls

"The wellsprings of the heart are awakened to compassion as one reads this book....The reader walks with and 'suffers with' the author as she shares the rich and many experiences of her life and service in the church....Instructive and inspirational."

Agnes Cunningham, S.S.C.M., Mundelein Seminary

"The lives and experiences of real people are presented in a way that allows the reader to see the holiness, the strength, and the conversion within each person. You begin to feel that wholeness and spiritual growth for *A Spirituality of Compassion*. It deserves to be read and then read again."

Bishop Thomas J. Gumbleton, Archdiocese of Detroit

"Joan Puls's thoughtful meditations on spirituality, faith, and justice help to restore some dignity to the word 'compassion.' She knows there is no real feeling without suffering, no knowledge without work....*A Spirituality of Compassion* is no vague sermon about 'loving and sharing.' It is wise counsel, based upon concrete experience, re-created for us in language of simplicity and strength."

Michael True, Author of *Justice Seekers, Peace Makers*

"*A Spirituality of Compassion* is an excellent example of a book that holds Scripture and sacred tradition in one hand, the contemporary world in the other, and says, 'Get to know each other.'...A warm, challenging, and—in the best sense of the word—inspiring book."

Mitch Finley, *Praying*

"A book that not only should be *read* by every Christian, but a book that should be *written* by everyone of us who call ourselves followers of Jesus....This book can be reflected on, shared, and rewritten by us according to our personal experiences of graced life."

Clara Fehringer, O.S.U., *Sisters Today*

"Joan Puls has a special gift for interspersing anecdotes and reminiscences with challenging reflections on global outlook and a passionate commitment to justice and peace, helps to make this volume an outstanding work."

Thomas E. Clarke, S.J., International Bulletin of Missionary Research

Critical Acclaim for...*Every Bush is Burning: A Spirituality for Our Time* by Joan Puls

"Seeing the world, nature, communities and persons as infused with God's presence, Puls offers a view of life as sacramental and whole, juxtaposing modern living and gospel values."

Books and Religion

"Joan Puls certainly has a way with words, can create unusual figures of speech and is obviously widely traveled and widely read. The combination of these things, and her felicitous style, make for spiritual reading that is pleasant, powerful, and purposeful."

The Tablet

"Joan Puls describes a spirituality that is 'ordinary' and 'everyday.' The approach is profoundly incarnational, vividly personal, and global at the same time. This book encompasses the aspects and stages recognized as traditional in Christian spirituality; yet it is story rather than theory, or better, story with theory which real life itself furnishes. The gifts of women in society are strongly affirmed; yet the author also notes that the richness of the feminine spirit is not synonymous with the female person. In the end, the reader discovers in *Every Bush is Burning* that all authentic spiritual experience converges on one basic human yearning; the quest for fullness and meaning for all women and men."

Daniel DiDomizio, *Horizons*

"*Every Bush is Burning* is the very best kind of spiritual reading—the kind you have to put down every few pages in order to savor, ponder, and reflect, the kind that urges you to keep on in the cultivation of an inner life, to open yourself further to the hidden and the unexpected. This book is a lively, thorough development of an incarnational approach to living and praying. Joan Puls writes out of her own varied experience. She looks with the contemplative's eye at current events, finding God alive and working in the world. Her treatment of the role which conflict plays in the spiritual life is excellent. Crisis, she says, opens our eyes, forces us to re-evaluate, to go deeper into things. Conflict leads us to the gospels and to reliance on a faith community. Sister Joan's book is indeed a spirituality for our times.

Praying